Canoeing Complete

CANOE TYPES

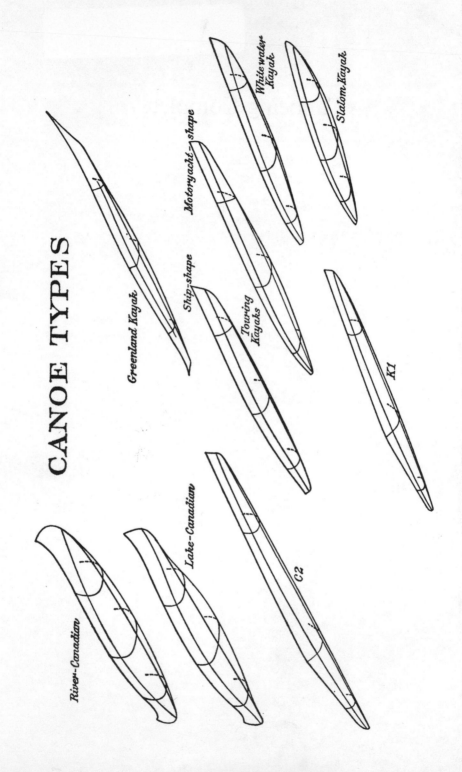

River-Canadian

Lake-Canadian

Greenland Kayak

Ship-shape

Motoryacht-shape

Touring Kayaks

Whitewater Kayak

Slalom Kayak

K1

C2

CANOEING COMPLETE

Edited by Brian Skilling, assisted by David Sutcliffe

With contributions by
Alan Byde, Oliver Cock, Jorgen Samson,
Geoffrey Sanders, Julian Shaw, Norman Sudron,
Kathleen Tootill and Marianne Tucker

Foreword by
Rear-Admiral Desmond Hoare (Retd)

36 *line and* 32 *half-tone illustrations*

NICHOLAS KAYE
LONDON

First published by
NICHOLAS KAYE LIMITED
2nd Impression
Kaye & Ward Ltd,
194–200 Bishopsgate, London EC2
1968

Printed in England by
C. Tinling & Co. Ltd,
Liverpool, London and Prescot

Contents

List of Illustrations

PHOTOGRAPHS

PHOTOGRAPHS

Between pages 176 and 177

DRAWINGS

DRAWINGS

ACKNOWLEDGMENTS

For their permission to reproduce illustrations, the editors wish to thank the following:

PHOTOGRAPHS

Aqua-photo Publicity—Nos. 3, 7–13, 16; Mr E. Boesch—No. 1; Streamlyte—No. 2; Mr J. H. Haward—Nos. 4 & 6; Mr D. Winning —No. 5; Mr S. K. Fraser—No. 14; Atlantic College—Nos. 17–32; Mr E. Lewis—No. 15.

DRAWINGS

Mr A. J. Appleby—Figs. 9–15; Mr Charles White—Figs. 16–23; Aqua-photo Publicity—Fig. 24; Mr Bryan Woods—Fig. 25; The British Canoe Union—Fig. 26.

Foreword

Rear-Admiral Desmond Hoare (Retd)
Headmaster, Atlantic College

PEOPLE sometimes talk about the explosive growth of canoeing in Britain. I do not believe that we have yet seen more than a beginning. Being of a statistical turn of mind I have examined over the last 12 years in three different situations the potential attraction of the sport to the age group of sixteen to eighteen. The three situations have been boys and apprentices in the Royal Navy, boys' club members in London clubs whose academic prowess rarely reached one Ordinary Level subject pass in the General Certificate of Education, and boys in the Atlantic College, all of whom are studying at Advanced Level for university entrance. In each of these three areas when canoeing has been offered in a sensible and efficient way, between two and three out of every ten boys have taken to it with enthusiasm and more than one in ten has been as keen or keener at the end of two years than at the start. There seems no correlation between I.Q. and enjoyment of canoeing.

In the Atlantic College we have found that enthusiasm for canoeing is very evenly spread over a wide variety of nations including Norway, Sweden, Denmark, Germany and Canada. I am not sure whether it is statistically safe to add that boys from warmer countries seem a little less ready to Eskimo roll in our waters.

I have had the opportunity in the same three areas of experience to compare enthusiasm for canoeing amongst this age group with enthusiasm for sailing. In the boys' clubs with equal efficiency of presentation, the canoe wins handsomely and in this College the numbers, after two years, are about equal. Sailing has a longer and wider tradition in Britain and we have to develop canoeing without the advantage of prestige and wealth at the top which yachtsmen enjoy. Nevertheless, develop it we must for the enjoyment of youth. Two hundred thousand boy and girl canoeists under the age of twenty is the kind of figure for which we should be planning. We must think in

terms of coaching 50,000 a year and we must see to it that
they are well and safely trained.

No matter in what kind of a craft one goes afloat, the chances
are that sooner or later one will be swimming; ability to swim
should be an absolute prerequisite to canoeing. It is always
sound to use national standards and the Amateur Swimming
Association Personal Survival Test at Bronze Level is a good
standard to adopt.

One can also make a convincing case for a first-aid qualifica-
tion, certainly for confidence in the artificial respiration of
others, and indeed in all three 'Bs', breathing, bleeding and
beating. The national first-aid societies offer sensible standards
to adopt. The size of the whole training task which faces our
mature canoeists seems daunting, but there arrives a time in
everyone's life when it becomes as much fun to teach as to
canoe, and the number of mature canoeists is beginning to
expand rapidly. We need well-thought-out courses, well staffed,
in teacher training colleges, especially, but by no means only
in those concerned with physical education, and they should
accept youth club leaders as extra mural students. We need a
great expansion of the canoe life guard scheme, training
schemes, technical committees, safety and accident investigation
committees as well as our pressure groups over water rights.
We need our competitive apex to the sport, but it will be
strong only if we see that the base of the sport is well built.

Whenever one meets young canoeists on river or lake or
sea, one should ask them to what club they belong, and if they
don't belong to any, one should find out their nearest and
encourage them along.

We must also give our full backing to the British Canoe
Union as the administrative focus of our efforts.

Finally, we need to know what we are talking about. It
therefore gives me the greatest pleasure to introduce this guide.
It has been written by acknowledged experts in each branch of
a great activity offering pleasure and fibre to youth.

Introduction

IN 1865, John MacGregor set out in a canoe of his own design and paddled along a thousand miles of European waterways. This voyage, and his later ones on the Jordan and the Baltic, caught the public imagination, his books describing his adventures became best-sellers, and, perhaps most important of all, he founded a new sport—recreational canoeing.

Over the past hundred years, the sport of canoeing has passed through many phases. MacGregor envisaged the canoe as a small craft which could either be paddled or sailed, and which could provide accommodation afloat if desired, but his contemporaries found the sailing aspect more appealing, and so canoes became larger and heavier, the paddle being used only in an emergency when the wind failed. In the 1880s the introduction of the open Canadian-type canoe from North America brought a temporary revival of interest in paddling, but by the end of the century this had almost vanished except as a casual form of recreation. The sailing canoe continued to enjoy limited popularity, but the cost of these large craft meant that their use was confined to a well-to-do minority.

The twentieth century brought the invention of the collapsible kayak which could easily be transported, and after the First World War canoe touring became immensely popular, especially on the continent. In 1936, canoe paddling races were accepted as an Olympic sport, and paddling was back in favour—and as a pastime well within the reach of most young sportsmen. The expeditions, too, from 1930 to 1933 of Gino Watkins to Greenland; the knowledge and experience which he and other members of his parties gained in kayaking with the Eskimos; and the demonstrations given afterwards in this country of the Eskimo Roll, suggested, almost for the first time to Europeans, the real potential in difficult waters of the expert canoeist in a suitable craft, that (what the Eskimos had known for many years) the canoe hull, the canoeist himself and his paddle must be thought of as one tight-fitting, completely co-ordinated unit.

Although this lesson had not been learnt by the outbreak

of war, and indeed was not really followed up until the 1950s, the canoe proved invaluable for inshore reconnaissance of enemy coastlines, and the raid of Lt-Col Hasler with his 'cockleshell heroes' on the shipping at Bordeaux is one of the most famous of wartime small-craft exploits. After the war, canoeing as a sport continued to grow in popularity, but as more and more people began to own cars, the collapsible kayak gave way to the rigid kayak, often home-built and made of lath-and-canvas, plywood, and latterly of glass-fibre. Increasingly, schools and youth organizations have found in canoeing a pursuit which gives young people an admirable opportunity of developing their creative handicraft talents in canoe construction, and their physical skills in facing the numerous challenges offered by canoeing today.

The past few years have seen a strong growth in specialization, both in the type of craft used and in the skills which have been developed to achieve optimum performance. As a result, whilst the all-rounder can still derive pleasure from the sport practised at his own level, the experts in the various branches are specialists who have devoted themselves to reaching the peak in, for example, slalom, racing or canoe surfing. This is inevitable and good, but one unfortunate side-effect has been that no one person can hope to write with authority and from personal experience on all aspects of the sport. It was with this in mind that the editors conceived the idea of this book: to gather together a group of people who were all experienced leaders in their particular field, and to persuade them to write about it without, however, forgetting the newcomer who needs a more general introduction to the sport. In this way it was hoped to produce a book which could be both comprehensive and to some degree authoritative.

One type of canoe, the Canadian, is, however, mentioned only in the chapter on canoe design. The reason for this is that Canadian canoeing is still a minority activity in this country, and to have included it would have meant either reducing the space devoted to other topics, or increasing the price of the book. It was decided that neither of these courses was justified, not least because the subject has been outstandingly well covered in *Canoeing*, by Joseph L. Hasenfus (published by the American Red Cross, price 15s.), and more briefly in the booklet *Canadian Canoeing* (published by the British Canoe Union, price 3s. 6d.).

We hope with *Canoeing Complete* to impel acceptance of the fact that modern canoeing can no longer be adequately written about by a single author. If we are successful, we shall have set a valuable precedent and perhaps made something of a landmark in canoeing literature. We hope, too, that revised editions of this book may appear from time to time in which current experts will be invited to bring their fellow-canoeists, schools, youth groups, training colleges and the general public up-to-date on the latest developments in their own particular sphere of the sport.

Brian Skilling
David Sutcliffe

1

Canoe Design

JORGEN SAMSON

PADDLING is the oldest method of boat propulsion. The prehistoric man undoubtedly used a piece of a branch as a paddle, riding astride a tree-trunk. A few thousands of years later his palaeolithic descendant made the first improvement in canoe design, the dug-out, hollowed by means of fire and pointed at the ends by means of a stone axe.

In Europe, dug-outs were used everywhere and in Sweden the last 'ege' disappeared only 150 years ago. In Hungary real canoes, also kayaks, were used for exercise as early as 1625. The name comes from the Spanish *canoa* (parallels: French *canot* and German *Kahn*) and refers to a great many types, all being narrow and pointed in their ends. They are propelled with a paddle, single or double bladed without any support on the boat so that the man is facing forward.

The appearance of canoes has always been impressive. The famous Swedish artist, Albert Engström, was a great admirer of their shape. He kept two kayaks hanging under the ceiling in his atelier. 'One can sit for hours admiring the beauty in the lines,' he said.

Canoes, however, are not made exclusively for the eye; they are given their shape to fulfil the demands of performance which may differ considerably.

If a canoe builder tells you that his canoe is perfect for every purpose, then do not trust him. The true all-round canoe should be narrow and beamy, high and low built, flat and rockered and that is why he did not build it. On the other hand, his canoe could be just the boat you need, possessing most of the qualities which are essential to your particular purpose.

The shape and the material in a canoe is decided by its use; racing or touring, open or sheltered water, rapid rivers or calm lakes. Furthermore, canoeists are typical individualists, each with his personal taste and special demands. The writer

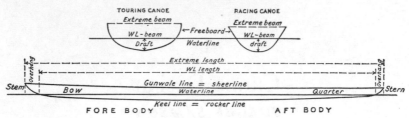

Fig. 2　Terms in canoe design

of this chapter also has his own ideas and prefers to express them definitely rather than trying to find the average meaning of the subject: the relationship between canoe form and performance.

Some abbreviations will probably be useful:

L—Length (maximum)

B—Beam (maximum)

LWL—Length on the waterline

BWL—Beam on the WL

WL—Waterline of the loaded canoe

DL—Draught, loaded

D—Displacement = Total weight of canoe, man and paddle

PC—Prismatic coefficient = fineness of the canoe; can be expressed as a value derived from the formula:

$$\frac{D \text{ (in cubic feet)}}{\text{Area of the widest section (in square feet)} \times L \text{ (in feet)}} \text{ where}$$

a value of more than 0·55 indicates a full form and one below indicates a fine form in the sense that the canoe is narrow in its bow and quarter.

We will also have to use terms such as 'sheerline' and 'rocker' which mean the curvature of the gunwale and the keel (Fig. 2).

The performance of any canoe can be discussed only if we define the different qualities concerned.

STABILITY

Stability is the resistance against rolling and depends upon the location of the centre of gravity and the centre of buoyancy. If a boat is leaned so much that the former falls outside the latter, it will capsize (Fig. 3). Fortunately, this inconvenient behaviour can be counteracted in various ways:

V-*Shape* cross section can either be flat in its angle and
s a stability only little inferior to the U-form or it can be
r and unstable. The canoe is then felt to be top heavy
t is inclined to lie over on either side, obviously hating
pright position.

ne *Round Shape* cross section gives stability only if the ratio

$\dfrac{L}{L}$ is great enough, i.e. when the part of the section below

L makes a flat arch. Decreasing $\dfrac{BWL}{DL}$ to the value 2·0 means

true semi-circular cross section below WL, at which point
any stability is lost. Regardless of the form, this ratio should
never fall below 5·0 in touring canoes and 3·1 in racers.

Combinations of the above mentioned forms are common.
In touring canoes the U-shape is given a flat V underneath
(Fig. 2). The result is more final than initial stability and a
limitation of buoyancy. All modern racing canoes are V-shaped
above the WL and round below and the stability, particularly
the final part, is very poor.

The rocker will also influence stability. A small amount of

rocker will decrease stability because of the small $\dfrac{BWL}{DL}$ ratio in

bow and quarter. A large amount of rocker has the opposite
effect and will also lower the centre of gravity a little.

SEAWORTHINESS

Seaworthiness is the ability to maintain stability, speed and
course in a scaway. A canoe which is stable in calm water is not
unconditionally safe in the sea. If it were so, we should expect
to find the maximum of safety in a beamy Canadian touring
canoe. This type, however, while highly regarded on inland
water, is not considered safe enough on the open sea.

The Canadian has much buoyancy and little draught. This
makes it skid or yaw in solid following waves and in spite of
its stability it cannot be considered a safe sea boat.

The touring kayaks are the superior craft for open sea
canoeing, but the most beamy of them are difficult to handle in
a strong wind and waves.

The U-shape, if beamy and flat, is so stable that it will follow
the profile of any wave coming from the side. This is felt in a

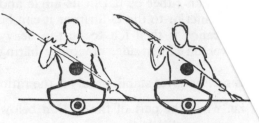

Fig. 3   Stability

1. Keep the centre of gravity low—simply b

2. Choose a canoe in which the centre of b
much when it is leaned. In other words, ch
canoe in which the submerged side is buoyant en
the rolling.

3. Move the centre of gravity with your body o
leaning.

In a C1 (racing Canadian canoe) the lack of sta
evident, it would roll over if the paddler was stiff like
He is not, however, and his ability to balance his body n
up for the lack of natural stability of the canoe. This exan
is the most extreme we have, but we face what is special
canoeing. The canoe itself cannot fully support its paddle
when leaned, for instance, in waves. To achieve full support
we need a beam of at least 40 inches and the canoe has changed
to a dinghy.

In a tippy racing canoe the sector of stability is very small
so that quick reactions are essential. In the beamy touring
canoe there is more time to react, but in both cases the canoeist
moves his body instinctively.

It is seen that beam makes for stability and, of course, it
also gives buoyancy. The resulting shape might be an 'airship',
easy for wind and waves to handle, but difficult and tiresome
for the canoeist. This factor, however, belongs to the seaworthiness and we will return to it later.

Within a certain beam the shape of the sections can vary
greatly and the difference in stability is considerable.

The U—or Box-Shape cross section gives most stability as
the centre of buoyancy moves much when leaning the canoe.
If the U-shape is used in narrow kayaks under 53 cm. beam
they feel safe because of a good initial stability, but their final
stability is relatively small.

B

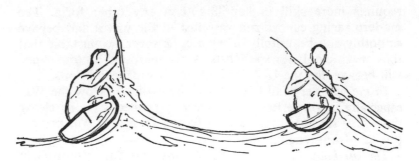

Fig. 4   The U-shape in a strong wind and waves

hard rolling tendency and if a wave is breaking just on your side, you will have a big job to do. First, by leaning your body very hard against the breaker in order to sustain the heel which tends to be as steep as the wave; next, when the wave has passed you must immediately change your weight over to the opposite side in order not to fall out of the canoe. In fact, it is easier to control a boat which is not quite as stable (Fig. 4).

The V-shape reduces the buoyancy and the initial stability and it also contributes to good directional stability. The latter is important, especially when the waves are coming on the quarter. Waves from this direction cause much more trouble than a true following sea as the canoe is constantly 'broaching to', i.e., turning parallel to the waves (Fig. 5). In these circumstances, a flat bottom with excessive rocker can be dangerous even if the canoe is felt to be stable enough.

A small amount of rocker is advisable and the sections should be sharp at the keel, at least in the bow and the quarter. An external keel is also helpful in order to establish the desired grip on the water.

The round form gives soft movements in side waves, but

Fig. 5   The V-shape in a strong wind and waves

requires more skill in handling than any other form. The modern racing canoes run very fast in the waves and behave smoothly and beautifully. They are, however, so unstable that they are safe only for specialists. A beamy round-bottom canoe will behave like the U-shaped one in all wave conditions.

In the bow very full lines should be avoided below the WL, especially in rockerless boats. Deep V-shaped sections cleave the waves smoothly and a high flaring freeboard will prevent the bow from digging too deeply.

The aft body in the past was beamy and flat (motor-yacht shaped, see frontispiece 'Canoe Types'), but because of the yawing tendency in a following sea this shape is not popular today. Instead, a rather full form with a cross section compromising the V and the round shape is used. The freeboard aft should be low.

The sheerline in the touring Canadian canoe is curved intensely near the ends. This is due to the fact that the boat is open; if decked like the kayaks there would be no risk of becoming swamped. In the latter, water can get inside only through the cockpit and the kayak must be high and buoyant at its middle in order to keep dry when riding on the crest of a wave. A spray cover eliminates swamping, but can feel uncomfortable to the canoeist as to some degree it hampers his movements and very soon will cause damp and moisture inside the hull. A weak sheerline curve is accordingly preferable in kayaks—it also lessens the windage.

The wind drift is considerable in beamy, high-built canoes. Thus the touring Canadian will scarcely make any advance in a strong wind if paddled only by one person. The steering is also heavily affected and the rudderless Canadian will soon teach us what happens in a wind. By trimming the canoe low at the stern, it turns away from the wind and conversely it turns against the wind when trimmed low in the bow. When at speed, nearly all canoes tend to turn against that side from which the wind is blowing and, as has been shown, the remedy is a low aft body.

The stem and stern profile acts on the sections in such a manner that a vertical stem tends to narrowness below the WL, whereas a marked overhang makes for blunt sections. For this reason, and also to reduce the wind drift, exaggerations in overhang should be avoided.

SPEED

Naturally speed is a question of water resistance of which the main part—75-90 per cent—is caused simply by friction between hull and water. The highest percentage is found at the lowest speed.

The frictional resistance depends on the size and the condition of the surface below the WL and increases with the speed. A minimum of 'wetted surface' can be achieved in a short deep hull with sections of true semi-circular form below the WL. In order to keep them semi-circular all the way, however, a large amount of rocker must be added, otherwise the boat will draw too deep at the stem and stern and thus again add to the wetted surface. A boat such as this is never built, as its stability is nil and as length and rocker have other functions of opposite demands. An approximation to the semi-circular form, where $\frac{BWL}{DL}$ is 3·4-3·0 has proved most efficient and is common in the modern racing canoes. V and U shaped sections will increase the wetted surface about 5 and 2 per cent respectively.

With regard to the condition of the surface of the hull, absolute smoothness is essential and grains of dust or sand in the varnish must be avoided. A coat of wax, oil, soap, in order to reduce friction, is useless.

The remaining 10-25 per cent of the resistance represents the energy lost by the creation of waves at bow and stern. By the way, this lost energy may be picked up again—by another competitor 'hanging on the wave' of the canoe in front of him. This *wave resistance* is also called the form resistance because it depends upon the form of any boat. It has little effect at low speeds but as the hull moves more quickly it increases more rapidly than the frictional resistance. In fact, the difference in performance of two models is usually due to the amount of wave resistance. To reduce wave resistance, the best remedy is to increase the length followed by decreasing the beam and achieving a correct prismatic coefficient.

Any canoe can be propelled with a very small amount of effort until a speed of about 4 knots. Up to this point only the frictional resistance counts: the wave resistance is negligible. The bow wave is low and short and there is no marked hollow behind it (Fig. 6a).

Fig. 6   Wave resistance

Above 5-6 knots the wave resistance grows rapidly. The bow wave becomes heavy and so long that the stern drops in the hollow behind it (Fig. 6b). When the level rises again behind the canoe, the stern wave is superimposed on its top and the result is a smooth transverse wave usable for 'hanging'.

At about 8 knots the wave now stretches to the middle of the canoe where a big beam would heavily increase the disturbance of the water. The transverse wave is heavy and comes up far behind the canoe, ideal for 'hanging'. The change of trim is most marked at this speed (Fig. 6c).

Ten knots will bring the crest of the wave near to the middle of the boat and the heavy aft trim starts to decrease again (Fig. 6d). If there was power enough to make a further 3 knots, the canoe would plane in front of its own bow wave.

Regardless of the size of the boat the wave length depends only on the speed. Accordingly, the wave phenomena just mentioned will appear at higher speeds in each case if the boat becomes longer. For a 17-foot boat, 5·5 knots is called the 'squatting speed' where the unfavourable wave pattern begins to manifest itself. For a 21-foot boat, this will occur at one knot more speed. Another reason why length will pay is due to the lower waves produced when the displacement is spread over a long hull. A high PC (above 0·6) contributes to speed in the same way.

For planing, however, length is unfavourable. On the figures given the canoe was suggested to be 17 feet, whereas 12 feet would give planing conditions at 10 instead of 13 knots. Unfortunately, this speed is never achieved as the resistance at the lower speeds is too great in a 12-footer. Every imaginable experiment has been tried out, but the lack of horsepower is evident. Experience has proved the best performance to be with a form where the planing features were modified to such a degree that none of the other speed-making factors were affected. This is, however, a problem only in racing canoes.

The touring canoes never achieve this 'squatting speed' in their ordinary use.

MANŒUVRABILITY

Manœuvrability is the ability of a canoe to change its course quickly and is mostly required in inland canoeing. On lakes and easy rivers a normal touring canoe will serve well, but for rapid rivers, blocked more or less with rocks, a special type of canoe is necessary. In such 'white water canoes' and still more in the slalom canoes, the manœuvrability has been developed to its fullest extent. This is only possible at the expense of other aspects of performance.

For a fast turn, a short hull with a small draught specially at the ends is essential. We have seen that such a form performs very badly in a seaway and the speed is also heavily affected.

The different demands of manœuvrability is dividing canoes into racing and open sea types with a long hull and a small amount of rocker, and the white water canoes of the opposite form, short hull and much rocker. Between these main groups a great many canoes of compromise form are found. Most of them are excellent for average conditions, but they should never be used for open sea, or white water canoeing.

A *rudder* is impracticable in a strong current, but it is very suitable for the directionally stable cruising and racing kayaks. The hinged stern rudder which is good for inland canoeing is unsuited for sea canoeing as in high waves it will occasionally be clear of the water. Here the fin rudder being attached one to two feet in front of the stern works perfectly, but it is liable to be easily damaged by obstructions in shallow water.

CANOE TYPES

Modern canoes are either the decked kayaks propelled with a double-bladed paddle, or Canadian canoes being open and single-bladed paddled. The kayaks are the faster and more seaworthy, but they require more skill in handling. In a Canadian canoe paddling is easily learnt and they are fairly stable and roomy. The kayak is primarily a single-seater, whereas the Canadian performs at its best as a double-seater.

The Touring Kayak

This developed from the Eskimo sealskin kayak which is still in use in Greenland and the arctic parts of Canada, Alaska and Siberia. Kayaks were first seen by Europeans when Greenland and Canada were discovered about the year 890. About 1450 some Greenland kayaks were shipped to Denmark and Norway and one was hanging in the dome of Trondheim for a long period. In 1801 a flotilla of kayakers was proposed to fight the British navy, but this plan was never realized—fortunately, you may say. During the last war British and Danish canoeists had the same enemy and in 1942 Lt-Col H. G. Hasler made his successful attack on ships in the port of Bordeaux.

About 1840 the first copies of Greenland kayaks appeared in Europe although in Hungary a domestic type at least 1,000 years old was still in existence. In our time the ancient European canoe types have completely disappeared, but copies of the Arctic ones are still built, mostly in the United Kingdom.

There are a great many types of Arctic kayaks, differing greatly from one place to another. The length can vary from 16 to more than 20 feet and the beam from 16 to 21 inches. The natives consider the long and narrow types as the most sea-worthy. The chine form is due to the frame construction and the basic shape is typified by the narrow ends, where the longitudinal lines sometimes have concave curves.

As kayaks are used for fishing and hunting among ice floes manoeuvrability is an important factor and consequently many kayaks, especially in sheltered water, are given a considerable amount of rocker. This further decreases the low PC and is the reason that most Greenland kayaks run easily only at low speeds.

The fore and aft sections are sharp at the keel and the chine, so that the kayak is not inclined to yaw very much. In this way manoeuvrability is combined with seaworthiness. The latter is further improved by the long overhanging stem profiles which increase the buoyancy as well as the directional stability when immersed in the waves.

After 1865 canoeing began to rise as a new kind of sport. The Scot, McGregor, made his sensational voyages in kayaks of his own design. These Rob-Roys were more ship-shaped than the Arctic types. The basic form was a box-shaped middle part running into a moderately rounded V-shape in the bow and quarter sections.

The Rob-Roys were comparatively short and beamy, L:15 feet, B:28 inches, but because of the short overhang and the flat curve of rocker, they utilized their length better than the Arctic types. Primarily McGregor's kayaks were much more stable and they were also rather faster because of their better PC. In rough water the Arctic types performed better, but they required too much skill in handling to contribute much to the growth of canoeing. The Rob-Roy type spread to the continent, starting the sport of canoeing in many countries.

About 1910 a new shape appeared in Sweden, being adapted from the motor-yacht. The idea was to cleave the water vertically with a deep, narrow bow and let it leave again horizontally under a flat beamy quarter. This shape was claimed to be speedy and seaworthy at the same time, but the higher speed was gained from more length and less beam and not from the shape. When heading into the waves, these kayaks behaved excellently, but in a following sea they could scarcely be worse.

Today touring kayaks are again 'double ended', being only a little fuller aft than fore. The single-seater above 16 feet is faster and moves more smoothly in the waves than the 15-footer which, in turn, is less awash. In my opinion 24 inches gives a sufficient beam for the long types and one inch more is enough for the short one. The speed is normally 4·5–5·0 knots. The double-seater makes one knot more—L:17–19 feet, B:26–28 inches.

The details of the shape depend on the use and the demands of the individual and refer to the performance concerned. New features from the racing canoes like the narrow fore body must soon influence the touring kayaks as the greater freedom of movement is also of benefit to the touring canoeist.

The Touring Canadian Canoe
This type originated from the birch-bark canoes used by the Indians in North America. The prototypes may be divided into two groups: a river type with very high freeboard at the stem and stern, good for foamy rivers; and another type with a more moderately curved sheerline made for lakes and coastal waters. There the high type caused trouble in the wind. An approach was also made to the decked kayaks far north in Alaska and on the Aleutian Islands.

As might be expected, the first use of Canadian canoes for sport and pleasure was in their native countries—Canada and

U.S.A. Very soon boat-builders started producing them commercially and in Chicago hundreds of timber Canadian canoes had been built by 1881.

The touring Canadians cannot develop much without losing their special features, i.e., they should be open, beamy and possess the high arched stems. The basic form belongs to the ship-shape we noticed in the Rob-Roys.

The river canoe is so rockered that it will lose too much buoyancy near its ends if this is not compensated by means of full lines. Equipped with a full-length spray cover, this type is serviceable for very fast rivers, but it is tiring for the canoeist on a straight course.

The lake canoe is directionally stable by being rockerless and the deep stem sections require fineness to such an extent that the horizontal lines are usually concave near the ends. This must, however, not be exaggerated. Paddled by two persons, one in each end, the lake Canadian is sufficiently manœuvrable, also on rivers if they are not too fast.

For coastal canoeing bilge keels and a spray cover will to some degree increase the seaworthiness, but the kayak always performs much better, and is safer.

The great advantage of the Canadian is the practicability of sleeping in them. With a beam of 36 inches there is room enough for two persons, and a tent-like cover can easily be raised over a number of arched hoops extending partly or entirely the length of the canoe as preferred. The length of such a 'cabin-cruiser' should be about 16 feet—the river type 14–15 feet. The speed is approximately 3·5 knots (Fig. 7).

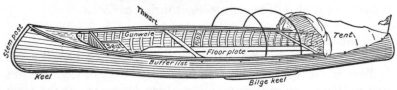

Fig. 7 The touring Canadian. In England the part designated as 'buffer list' is known as a 'rubbing stroke'

The White Water Canoes

These are the rockered variants of the short touring types we have discussed already. They are usually built for racing in accordance with international rules. Besides manœuvrability and speed the stability is also an important factor so that they are used for touring as well. Some ability to keep the course is advantageous and this is the reason why many canoeists prefer the old folding boats where the chines offer steadiness. This, however, has gradually been achieved in the glass-fibre boats by means of slightly deeper and more V-shaped sections fore and aft. Softly curved stem profiles prevent damage from obstructions in the water. Many models are surprisingly low at the bow so that the water first flows away near the cockpit where the deck is raised to a considerable height. A moderately curved sheerline, combined with a more horizontal shape of the deck, would certainly perform better.

The Slalom Canoes

Slalom canoes are so specialized that it is difficult to maintain a straight course in them. They react immediately to the paddle strokes in any direction desired, even sideways. They are shorter than 14 feet, being narrower and more rockered than the white water canoes. Consequently, unusually full lines are essential and they are nowadays worked into the hull and the deck as well. In order not to touch the hanging poles of the slalom gates, the boats are very low built. The rocker is curved most intensively near the ends running smoothly to the stem heads. The sections are round, or U-shaped.

The Racing Canoes

Canoe racing started between 1860 and 1870 and for many years each country used its own type, Greenland kayaks, custom types, or Rob-Roys. Racing shells from the rowing sport were also used, but about 1910 the motor-yacht-shaped type of Swedish design (see frontispiece) began to spread. The measurements from these kayaks were used for the rules when the International Canoe Federation started in 1924. In the 1930s the fish-shape was dominant for some years and then there was a change to more symmetrical hulls. The sections changed from U to V and narrow unstable boats appeared first in kayaks and then also within the Canadian type. In 1956 concave sections were introduced in order to reduce the WL-beam. This was possible already by means of the V-shape, especially if the canoes were high built, but low hulls with round sections provided a better solution. In the round form the wetted surface is smaller, but the hull much beamier. Concave sections or high flaring freeboards make it possible to decrease the beam and while concavity was banned from 1963 the other remedy is still legal (Fig. 2).

Today, freedom for movement during the paddle strokes grows more and more important due to the advances in paddling technique. Consequently, the widest point of the canoes is located so far aft that they are very narrow at their bow and middle part. At the widest point the freeboard is so high that the width can be worked away above the WL.

The narrow bow develops until there is just room enough for the canoeist. Unfortunately, the speed in rough water and even also in calm water is affected by this. The PC tends to be too low, planing effect no longer exists and the buoyancy is kept within a larger wetted surface than before. The solution to this problem is to add buoyancy to the bow below the gunwale, and at the same time to keep the narrowness where it is advantageous to the paddle work. In the latest canoes the bow sections are continuing edgeless into the deck and the arched freeboards are deflecting the bow wave much better than the earlier vertical ones (Fig. 8).

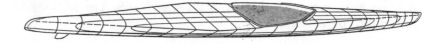

Fig. 8   Modifications to the racing canoe

In racing canoes only the speed counts, but as speed also includes rough water performance, seaworthiness comes into consideration. Due to the high speed and the long narrow hull, racing canoes cut through the waves rather than climb over them. In rough water they are almost constantly awash and even in the wake from competitors the deck occasionally cleaves the water. To avoid this, we need extremely high freeboards but as the wind resistance must be the lowest possible they have never been introduced. Instead, the shape of the deck is modified and slalom and racing canoes have found buoyant deck sections and edgeless gunwales.

The racing kayaks include K1, K2 and K4. Earlier the size of wetted surface was considered as being nearly fixed and almost impossible to bring down. Nevertheless, it has decreased about 6 per cent compared with the 1950 boats. The remedy was round narrow sections, $\dfrac{\text{BWL}}{\text{DWL}}$ being 3·0–3·2. A still narrower and deeper section is too unstable and has proved no advantage in speed. Rocker generally decreases the wetted surface but increases the change of trim. A rocker line being flat at its middle and curved more and more intensively towards the ends provides the best results. The K1 is specially sensitive to changes in the rocker—a quarter of an inch can be felt in performance. Too much makes the kayak bounce in the spurts, and too little makes it feel 'dead' and harsh running over the racing distances.

Planing features such as deep and flat aft sections are efficient only to a smooth paddling style. In the latest K1 and K2 planing forms only exist in so far as the centre of buoyancy is worked deeper in the hull towards the stern, i.e., the bow has fuller form above the WL and the quarter is fuller in or below the WL. This does not agree with the modern narrow form unless we use the arched freeboards previously mentioned. In a K4 no planing or lifting effect is possible: here the frictional resistance is still more important than in the K1 and K2.

K1—L. (max.) 520 cm., B. (min.) 51 cm., Weight (min.). 12 kg. Highest speed: 10,000 m. 7·2 knots: 1,000 m. 8·2 kn.: 500 m. 8·8 kn.: Spurts 10.0kn.

K2—L. (max.) 650 cm., B. (min.) 55 cm., Weight (min.) 18 kg. Speed: 10,000 m. 7·8 kn.: 1,000 m. 8·9 kn.: 500 m. 9·7 kn.: Spurts 11·5 kn.

K4—L. (max.) 1,100 cm., B. (min.) 60 cm., Weight (min.) 30 kg. Speed: 10,000 m. 8·6 kn.: 1,000 m. 10·0 kn.: 500 m. 10·8 kn.

The racing Canadian canoes C1 and C2 began developing later than the kayaks, but then continued until they had not the slightest likeness with traditional Canadian canoes. All that is left is the Canadian beam of 75 cm. being located like a sort of rudiment far aft and high above the WL. In my opinion, the Canadian canoe should never have been the prototype for single-bladed paddling. Look at the overgrown C8 being 3 feet wide, and compare it with the low and narrow South Sea war canoe! In a racing single canoe 75 cm. is also an enormous width, only doing harm to the steering. The beam can be measured anywhere on the canoe and so it only influences the gunwale shape, whereas below the WL the canoes are exactly as narrow as the kayaks. They only differ by being rockerless and in that a small amount of V-shape is often added to the bottom of the round sections, especially in the quarter. Even if this means a larger wetted surface the directional stability gained is essential to the steering. Turns are made by leaning the canoe. The height at the widest point is necessary for this reason as well as to get a small WL beam. If not counterbalanced by means of a very low stern, this height makes for trouble in steering with the wind on the side.

C1—L. (max.) 520 cm., B. (min.) 75 cm., Weight (min.) 16 kg. Speed: 10,000 m. 6·0 kn.: 1,000 m. 7·2 kn.: 500 m. 7·8 kn.

C2—L. (max.) 650 cm., B. (min.) 75 cm., Weight (min.) 20 kg. Speed: 10,000 m. 7·0 kn.: 1,000 m. 8·1 kn.: 500 m. 8·6 kn.

C8 (not accepted for international championships)—L. (max.) 1,100 cm., B. (min.) 93 cm. The speed is nearly that of a K1.

A rudder is legal on kayaks whereas no kind of steering mechanism is allowed in Canadians. If fitted, an external keel shall be straight and the two halves of any cross section when divided by a vertical centre line shall be symmetrical. The deck, if any, shall leave 295 cm. free of a C1 and C2 regardless.

2

Basic Technique

GEOFFREY SANDERS

WHEN practised sensibly, canoeing is a comparatively safe sport. Good instruction in the basic techniques will play an important part in producing a careful and reasonable approach to the sport, because it will enable the beginner to know and appreciate his own limitations and those of the canoes he uses.

To this end it is recommended that where possible the newcomer should either attend a course for beginners or obtain tuition from someone who is qualified to give it. However, material in this chapter is meant for the novice: it is hoped that those able to attend courses will find it useful for preliminary reading or possibly for revision, whilst the beginner who has to teach himself will find it provides a workable basis for self-instruction. For the beginner, especially, there are three preliminary points that must be made.

1. Don't canoe if you are unable to swim.

2. Wear an approved life-jacket and make sure that you know how to put it on correctly.

3. Never go out alone. If it is impossible to get another canoeist to go with you for your first venture afloat, take a sensible friend who can swim. Work out with him beforehand what you will do in the event of a capsize. Study Chapter 8— Oliver Cock on 'Safety in Canoeing'—carefully before you start, checking that the necessary conditions are fulfilled. If your friend has this book with him he might well be able to assist in the instruction by reading out the appropriate commentary.

A. INITIAL TECHNIQUES

For the first practical session we need a nice, easy bank, not more than a foot or two high, and a calm stretch of water. Anything that may produce an unplanned capsize is to be shunned, be it underwater obstacle or overhanging trees. Although trees may look picturesque their branches are only too willing to ensnare the innocent beginner. A capsize will be an essential part of the early instruction—but only when directed! Common sense suggests that the scene of your first introduction into a canoe should be well clear of weirs, rapids, mud flats, and the like, where you could so easily get into difficulties.

Check that you have all your personal gear with you. Apart from your 'travelling' clothes you will need a towel and two sets of canoeing clothes. Make sure that there are some warm garments amongst them—the water may be cold and you will be glad of them after the capsize drill has been practised. Recommended canoeing wear—depending on the weather— includes swimming kit, shorts, vest or singlet ('T' or games type), a sweater or pullover (preferably not a windcheater or track suit as they tend to hold the water and are heavy when wet), anorak or smock. A pair of plastic sandals or cheap gym shoes should be worn on the feet.

1. Carrying the Canoe

Carrying the canoe to the water is a game that one, two, four or six can play! The purpose of the manœuvre is not only that the boat should be transported from point 'A' to point 'B' but also that it should arrive intact. It is probably true that more damage takes place to boats *out* of the water than in the water —simply because they are not handled carefully and correctly. I have seen a canoeist pull a canoe across a field by its painter: another carried the boat on his shoulder but didn't seem to mind that the stern was periodically bouncing off the ground. Good habits for handling canoes out of the water as well as in it should be encouraged from the very beginning.

It is unwise to carry a fully loaded canoe unless there are enough helpers to ensure that it can be carried safely. A loaded double may require as many as four or six people to carry it— one at each end and one or two on each side of the cockpit. An unladened single can be carried with ease by two, with one person holding each end nestled comfortably under his arm. The hand should grasp the keel and rest against the hip. For short portages it is possible to carry the boat on your own. If the distance to be covered is only a few yards, the boat can be held with one arm under the near side of the cockpit with the

1. A K2 drives through the water towards the end of a long distance race at Oxford

2. The Telemark turn. Note the reversed left wrist, the pressure the canoeist is exerting with his right hand, the way he is looking behind him, and the speed with which the stern is scudding sideways across the surface. Note, above all, the complete confidence the canoeist has in leaning his whole weight on his paddle blade

3. A clean gate!

weight of the boat taken by the hip. Alternatively, the canoe can
be carried on the shoulder—the point of balance of the cockpit
resting on the shoulder with the elbow and lower arm inside the
cockpit to give additional support. Other techniques can be
devised later, such as carrying the boat on the head . . . to be
watched when there are high winds!

2. Boat Inspection
Before launching the canoe you must always check that your
equipment is in order. There must be no loose ends of painters
left lying about the cockpit. Seats (and backrests if used) should
be firmly attached. Spare clothes, repair kits, etc., should be in
waterproof bags and tied into the canoe—making sure that no
gear is left cluttering the cockpit where it might obstruct an
easy exit in the event of a capsize. (Any heavy equipment should
not be placed in the canoe until it is on the water and securely
fastened to the bank.) Examine the boat's buoyancy to see that
it is adequately attached and inflated. The paddle should be
feathered correctly for your own use. (See later under 5b).
Before putting on your lifejacket, check that it is in sound order
and make sure that you adjust it correctly.

3. Launching
Care is needed in launching as well as carrying the boat. It is not
enough to slide it into the water: there may be sharp stones or
broken pieces of glass waiting to scratch if not tear the hull.
The canoe must never be moved whilst it is in contact with the
ground: if this simple rule is kept, there are many ways in which
the craft can be safely launched and removed from the water.
(a) *Two-man launch:* one at each side of the cockpit. Holding
the boat at 90 degrees to the bank, the stern is lowered into the
water and the rest of the canoe then 'handed down', keeping it
as low as possible to the bank without actually touching. The
bow is then manœuvred round so that it is facing upstream (or
against the wind) and the boat is parallel to the bank.
(b) *Single-man launch:* the canoe held at 90 degrees to the
bank either against the knees, with both hands holding the edge
of the cockpit, or on the hip, with a supporting arm in the
cockpit. The stern is lowered into the water as in the two-man
launch and pulled round until it is adjacent to the bank.
Variations on these methods are possible and often necessary
where the launching site is awkward. A modification of the

c

single-man launch, for example, is to hold the canoe across the thighs and to place it in the water parallel to the side. One hand holds the boat by the cockpit, the other the gunwale to prevent it from chafing the bank. If the boat is at all heavy, this method often requires more strength than a youngster possesses. A failure to calculate accurately the distance to the edge of the bank can also result in the launching of the canoeist as well as the canoe!

4. Embarkation

Before very long you will be entering your boat in many different ways as required by the situations of the moment and you will have forgotten your first uncertain seconds when trying to master the art. For a canoe, rather like a bicycle, needs to be approached with care. Once you have mastered the basic essentials, you can venture forth and experiment with new methods. In the initial instruction, therefore, perfect two methods of entry into the canoe—one from the land and the other from shallow water. Entry from overhanging trees and other applied gymnastic feats can be left until later!

There are two important things to remember:

(*a*) Until you are really competent, do everything *slowly* and deliberately.

(*b*) Where possible all parts of the anatomy should be kept *central* when coming into contact with the boat.

And now for the operation itself.

FROM THE BANK

(i) *Embarkation*

Let us imagine that you are standing on the bank, facing the bow of the boat which is in the water alongside and to your right.

(*a*) Kneel or crouch—with the cockpit of the canoe to your right.

(*b*) LEFT hand; clutching a clump of grass or flat on the ground. Keep it in this position until you are comfortably seated in the canoe—it will ensure your equilibrium, of mind as well as body!

RIGHT hand—to the front of the cockpit (or as near as you can reach it on the right-hand side if the cockpit is a long one).

Fig. 9   Embarkation from a bank

(*c*) RIGHT leg into the centre of the boat, leaving sufficient room between it and the seat for your other foot.

(*d*) LEFT hand remains on bank.
LEFT foot into canoe, behind right.

(*e*) LEFT hand remains on bank.
RIGHT hand on front of cockpit.
SLOWLY lower yourself into the seat.

(*f*) Make yourself comfortable. If you need to change your seating position remember that any movement must be a balanced movement. If your hands are to take your weight put them behind you—say, one on either side of the back of the cockpit. Remember that being comfortable in a canoe really means being a part of the canoe. Your feet should be against the footrest (you may have to disembark to adjust it); your knees pressed against the side of the underside of the cockpit (depending on the boat) and your seat secure, preferably with hip supports. A loose or wobbly seat is a possible source of danger and a hard, moulded seat, besides being better from the canoeing and safety points of view, is usually much more comfortable on a long journey.

Before disembarking test the *stability* of the boat . . . and yourself! Push off a little from the side, raise your hands above your head and rock the boat from side to side. Bend sideways from the hips to left and right and you will find that you can rock the boat to left and right with your knees and seat—provided that they are sufficiently well anchored in the boat.

Fig. 10   Embarkation from shallow water

Can you get water lapping into the cockpit without capsizing the canoe?

(ii) *Disembarkation*

Follow the reverse procedure to embarkation:

(*a*) LEFT hand to hold bank.

(*b*) Bring knees close up to body. RIGHT hand to front of cockpit.

(*c*) Feet still in the boat. Raise body until standing. LEFT hand still on the bank: RIGHT on front of the cockpit.

(*d*) LEFT foot out, followed by RIGHT.

FROM SHALLOW WATER

(i) *Embarkation*

There will be many occasions on shallow rivers where you will have to enter your boat from water up to knee depth. In a normal touring boat the procedure is as follows:

You are standing in the water by your boat, with the cockpit to your right.

(*a*) Place your RIGHT leg in the cockpit. (Shake mud, water etc. from the foot first.)

(*b*) Place both hands behind the body—position them one either side of the cockpit behind the seat.

(*c*) Take the weight of your body on the hands and, thus balanced, bring your left leg into the canoe. (Again, shake the foot dry if time allows.) Lower yourself into a comfortable sitting position.

(ii) *Disembarkation*

(*a*) Hands are placed behind the body on the back of the cockpit.

(*b*) Weight of the body taken by the hands.

(*d*) Left leg out—takes the weight of the body—hands can be moved, right one to front of cockpit—right leg follows.

In a canoe with a very small cockpit this method may not be practicable, as there will not be sufficient room to push the knees below the deck. Beginners with this kind of boat are advised to delay attempting embarkation from shallow water until they are really familiar with the boat. They will then be able to devise methods of entry—for example, using a modified 'bank' entry with the paddle serving as an outrigger.

Practise such methods of embarkation and disembarkation until you can do them·without thinking.

Now pull the canoe out of the water and we can introduce you to the paddle!

5. Paddling Strokes

HOLDING THE PADDLE

You can practise holding the paddle on dry land for a few moments to check that you grasp it in the correct fashion and have the right idea as far as the stroke is concerned. Many beginners have their wrists much too close together on the paddle. Support the paddle on your head with your elbows at right angles—this will give you about the right grip.

Use the blades feathered—that is, at right angles to each other—from the start. This makes for easier paddling in the long run. One hand is going to hold the paddle firmly; the wrist will, therefore, be doing a lot of the work when it twists the shaft of the paddle through the necessary 90 degrees. The shaft of the paddle is going to swivel through the other wrist and so obviously the grasp will not be such a tight one. Try this for yourself and watch the movement of the blades. Thumbs are under the shaft, by the way. Decide which wrist you prefer to do the work and, if the paddles are spooned, adjust them accordingly. Try a few 'fresh air' strokes and if all seems well you are ready for the water!

FORWARD PADDLING

Once you are afloat push away from the bank—with your hand and not the paddle. Check that your grip is correct in relation to the paddle blades. The stroke is a natural one, but there are three points that should be remembered. It should be a *LONG* stroke. Push one arm forward until it is straight in front and even then push it a little further by turning the shoulders. Don't let your wrist cross the centre line of the boat. Your other arm will, of course, be pulling back the other blade through the water until your wrist is more or less in line with the body and near the cockpit coaming. It is also a

LOW stroke. For normal cruising your pushing hand will go down towards the front of the cockpit rather than up towards the head. The paddle blades need not go much above your head. Furthermore let your first movements be

SLOW and deliberate. Don't rush them: work out each stroke carefully in your mind, especially as far as the feathering movement is concerned. Watch the blade in the water until you are sure that you automatically start the stroke correctly. At the point of entry the blade will be at an angle of about 45 degrees to the surface of the water, but after the initial few inches it will be at right angles—excepting again the last few inches of the stroke. See that only the blade and not the shaft of the paddle is immersed during the stroke.

PRACTISE until you find that you don't need to watch the blade each time that it enters the water . . . and then don't. There is nothing that looks quite so ungainly as the canoeist who turns his head every time he makes a stroke.

BACKWARD PADDLING

It is simply the reverse of forward paddling and as such does not require careful enumeration here. You make the stroke with the back of the blade and even if the blade is spooned you do not turn them. Watch the first few strokes to check on the correct angle of entry of the blade into the water. Remember . . . long . . . low . . . slow strokes!

STOPPING

There are no brakes in a canoe and it is impracticable to carry an anchor to throw out when you want to stop! Push the vertical paddle into the water, level with your body—first on one side and then on the other. If necessary, add a short backward stroke on each occasion. Be ready for the sudden braking, especially when travelling at a fair speed, by bracing yourself in the canoe.

TURNING

Turning will soon come naturally but it is useful in the early stages of instruction to practise deliberately the different turning methods. As in driving a car, always try to anticipate your moves well beforehand.

Right turn: an extra forward stroke on the left and/or a backward stroke on the right.

Left turn: an extra stroke on the right and/or a backward stroke on the left. (See also 'Sweep stroke' p. 42.)

FERRY GLIDE

A manœuvre which will enable you to put into practice some of the strokes you have already learnt, and which is to be considered essential for river canoeing, can now be introduced. Called the 'Ferry Glide', it enables the canoe to glide across the stream when it is desired to alter the course of the boat after some obstacle has been sighted ahead. It represents a way of using the power of the stream to move the boat sideways and can be used when proceeding upstream or downstream.

(i) *Downstream.* As soon as you see the obstacle:

(*a*) Effect one strong backward paddle stroke on the side you *don't* want to go. This will have the effect of slightly turning the bow of the boat at an angle to the current in the direction you *don't* want to go.

(*b*) Back paddle on the same side again and then on both sides alternately. The stream will carry the canoe across the stream in the desired direction. Continue back paddling until you see the clear passage ahead.

(ii) *Upstream.* As soon as you see that you have to change your course:

(*a*) Execute one strong forward paddle stroke on the side that you *don't* want to go. This will turn the bow in the direction that you *do want* to go.

(*b*) Give another forward stroke on the same side and then on both sides alternately. Continue forward paddling until you are far enough across the stream.

The strength of the current will determine the angle of the boat to the main stream, but beware at all costs of putting the boat broadside against the current. Quite a slight angle, say of 10

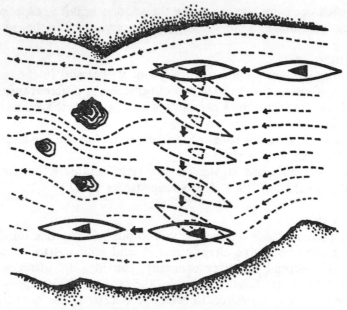

Fig. 11 Ferry Glide (facing downstream). The angle of the canoe is varied according to the speed of the current

degrees, will often suffice and experience will soon enable you to judge the right amount of strength to put into that initial stroke. It is a sound plan to practise ferry glides on every new piece of moving water that you attempt. You can even try out the initial emergency strokes on still water to show that you have got the right reaction. Many people have been taught the manœuvre on canals and have been able to apply what they have learnt on their first river trip.

PULLING INTO THE BANK

Here the paddle blade can be used as a rudder in order to turn the boat parallel to the bank. Experiment well away from the bank in the first instance. Push the paddle out just to the rear of your body with the blade, vertical in the water, at about 45 degrees to the boat. You may find it helpful to hold the shaft of the paddle against the side of the boat. If the canoe is moving when you make this 'stern rudder' stroke, it will have the effect of turning the bow towards the paddle side. Head the canoe towards the bank at an angle of about 45 degrees. Remember that you will want to land with the bow pointing upstream, or into the wind. As you approach the bank apply the 'stern rudder' on the opposite side of the boat to the bank. Practice will make perfect but, until it does so, avoid shortening the canoe by trying to widen the bank!

TWO-SEATER TECHNIQUES

I have assumed that the beginner is going to use a single-seater canoe. Even if he possesses a double there is much to be said in favour of his using it as a single for the initial stages of instruction. When it comes to be used by two people, there are additional factors that must be considered.

The stern man is the captain and is responsible for the control of the boat.

The bow man sets the stroke—long, low and slow to start with—and continues with this unless the captain orders otherwise. The bow man is in a much better position to see obstacles and he should pass the word back to the captain if he sights any; but the stern man is much better placed to take evasive action. The bow man can often continue with the normal paddling rhythm whilst the stern man, say, misses a stroke on one side or even applies a 'stern rudder' stroke. The bow man may be asked to apply a forward sweep stroke (described later on p. 42) whilst the stern man uses a backward sweep. Paddling must be synchronized—the paddles in unison and not simulating a windmill! The clashes (and cracks?) that the latter style will inevitably cause will not lead to harmony between the paddlers either! The more practice the pair can get together, the more effective will be the paddling.

This should provide sufficient instruction for your first session on the water. The important thing now is to try all these out for yourself and to become really familiar with the different skills. A short trip on calm waters can be recommended as it will enable you to become really familiar with the boat. Keep trying the turns in as many varied situations as you can find. Improvise a simple 'still water' slalom course where you can paddle round obstacles, paying more attention to style than speed at this stage.

If it is possible, I would strongly recommend that you practise a deliberate capsize at one stage during this first session afloat. It is an important safety drill and will also give you considerable confidence. You will learn to appreciate that a capsize is in no way to be feared in normal circumstances. The drill is explained by Oliver Cock in Chapter 8.

B. PROFICIENCY SKILLS

Instruction should not cease once you are able to paddle around, even if with a fair degree of competence. Although many who consider themselves to be proficient canoeists go no further than this, it is now generally recognized that further instruction is extremely valuable and is to be wholeheartedly encouraged. The canoeist himself will obtain greater enjoyment and gain new confidence from being able to exercise much greater control over his boat. This will stand him in good stead when he has to face difficult waters and hazards, and will give him a clearer insight into the capacities of the boat and his ability to handle it.

Two Preliminary Points
Before describing the different strokes, I should like you to note the following:

(*a*) The *hand position* on the paddles should remain as for normal paddling: the hands should not be moved into a positon that appears better for the particular stroke being attempted. Half the point of these basic strokes is that they can be used at any time—quickly—from the normal paddling position. If the paddles to be used for instruction are too long, it may be necessary to experiment with change of hand positions in order to get the feel of the stroke. If this is the case, obtain a shorter pair as soon as you can.

(*b*) You should now begin to try controlled '*leans*' in your canoe. As you paddle in a forward direction—without interrupting the continuity of the paddling and with your hips and lower body braced in the canoe—lean the boat to one side, keeping your trunk as upright as possible. Most canoes have a tendency to turn away from the lean. Experiment with the effects of leans—of both boat and body—in the different strokes. In the case of forward paddling, for example, you will have discovered a means of turning the boat without breaking the rhythm of paddling.

Sweep Strokes
The sweep stroke is a means of turning the boat more quickly, and is really an exaggerated turn stroke (described earlier). It can be used when the canoe is stationary or moving slowly. To turn the canoe a complete circle one keeps using a long forward

stroke (forward sweep) on one side and a long backward stroke (backward sweep) on the opposite side. For example, to turn the boat to the right or in a clockwise direction, lean and reach forward, letting the left blade enter the water vertically as near the bow as possible. Bring this blade round in a full arc until it is near the stern of the boat, by which time you should be leaning slightly backwards and towards the blade. Then turn the body to place the right blade in the water near the stern and bring it forwards in a wide circle to the bow.

Practise . . . first one way and then the other. How many strokes are required to turn the boat through 360 degrees? Can you improve on this by leaning a little further?

Fig. 12   Sweep stroke

Two Recovery Strokes

A canoeist will often be faced by situations when his balance is threatened. An unseen boulder may jar the hull of his canoe or an unexpected wave cause him to lurch perilously. The competent paddler will be able to remedy this at once by the quick application of a recovery stroke—using the paddle to push himself back into a position which enables him to resume full control of the boat.

RECOVERY BY SLAP SUPPORT

(1) *Starting position:* Brace yourself in the cockpit, leaning slightly forwards. Normal paddle grip. Paddle at right angles to the boat, just in front of the body. Blade just above and parallel to the water. Concave side upwards if using a curved blade.

(2) *Action:* Lean towards the blade and press firmly and sharply on the paddle to bring yourself to the vertical position again.

Note:—Paddle at right angles to the boat.
Blade flat on the water.
A firm, quick push.

(3) *Practice:* Tip the boat a little further each time until water is lapping round and into the cockpit. Try it on each side and, when you have got the knack of twisting the paddle to ensure that the blades are flat to the water, try a series of recovery strokes on alternate sides. When you feel really competent, ask someone to hold the stern of the boat and rock it unexpectedly to the left and right: see if you can prevent him from turning you out!

Fig. 13 Sculling for support

SCULLING FOR SUPPORT

(1) *Starting position:* Brace yourself in the cockpit, leaning slightly forwards. Normal paddle grip. Paddle pointing forwards at about 45 degrees to the boat. Paddle nearly flat on the water, the edge towards the stern of the boat being raised slightly (some 10 degrees). Concave side upwards if using a curved blade.

(2) *Action:* The paddle is going to be swept round in an arc for approximately 90 degrees, It will then be pointing towards the stern, at about 45 degrees to the boat. The edge of the blade that is 'leading the way' must always be slightly raised. Thus on the return stroke the other edge of the blade (i.e., the edge facing the bow) must be raised. The paddle is then kept moving continuously, the leading edge always being raised. If you have difficulty in knowing which way to twist the blade, remember that the same side of the paddle must always face the boat.

Try this slowly along the surface of the water, experimenting with the angle of the blade to the water, and turning the blade at the beginning and end of the arc. When you can do this without looking at the paddle, lean towards the blade in the water . . . further . . . and further . . . until the cockpit is awash. The blade will support you so long as you keep it moving and at the right angle to the water.

(3) *Practice:* Practice on both sides, seeing how far you can go! If you find yourself going too far and are in danger of capsizing, apply a quick recovery stroke by slap support in order to right yourself. A good canoeist will use one or other of these strokes, or a combination of both, to right himself in difficult moments. Imagine that you hit a submerged boulder at different moments of the normal paddling stroke and react accordingly. Ideally, practise these strokes at a time when a capsize is not too uncomfortable—a session in an indoor swimming pool in the winter can be very useful. If the thought of a capsize does not worry you, you will perfect these strokes much more quickly.

Two Sideways or Draw Strokes
It is desirable to be able to manœuvre the canoe into any required position. Draw strokes, therefore, should be mastered by the beginner who is anxious to feel that he is in full control of his boat. There will be many occasions, not only in slalom

competitions but also in general touring, when he will find it useful to be able to move the boat in a sideways direction.

DRAW STROKE

(1) *Starting position:* Brace yourself in the cockpit, leaning slightly forwards. Normal paddle grip. Paddle at right angles to the boat. Stretch the paddle over to one side—the blade near the water, parallel to and as far away from the boat as can be reached comfortably. Concave side of blade towards the canoe.

(2) *Action:* (*a*) Draw the paddle, blade fully covered, into the side of the boat. STOP when the blade is near (not touching) the boat and the paddle is vertical: to proceed further than this point will demonstrate how a paddle can lever you out of a canoe!

(*b*) Twist the blade through an angle of 90 degrees and slice it through the water back to the starting position. (Alternatively, the blade can be sliced out of the water, without

Fig. 14   Draw stroke

turning, towards the stern of the canoe and then carried through the air to the starting position. This method of recovery tends to be slower, however, and is not quite so neat).

(c) Having got the 'feel' of the stroke, lean towards the paddle—this will make the draw much more effective. Return to the vertical position just before the end of the actual draw stroke.

(3) *Practice:* Practise on both sides of the canoe, across the river or canal. If there are two canoes present, have a sideways race! Try the effect of the draw stroke not just with the paddle at 90 degrees to the boat but placed at different angles, both towards the bow and stern. Don't be satisfied until you can really lean into your stroke. The timing of this, of course, requires plenty of practice.

SCULLING DRAW

(1) *Starting position:* The beginner is advised to approach the sculling draw from the sculling-for-support stroke. Start with the paddle travelling in its arc to and fro along the surface of the water. There is no need to lean out on the paddle on this occasion as the stroke is not going to be used for support.

(2) *Action:* Continuing the movement of the stroke bring the blade in towards the side of the canoe—the blade out of the

Fig. 15 Sculling draw

water will thus move to a position where it is nearly vertical above the blade in the water. Keep the blade moving—it will be following the shape of a figure eight and will be moving the boat sideways towards the paddle. If this does not quite work out first time, go back to the sculling-for-support movement and try again. Examine the parts of the sculling draw stroke. Note how the leading edge of the blade is pointing away from the boat all the time. In order to achieve this, the angle of the paddle has to be changed continually. Experiment with different angles.

(*If you have the leading edge of the blade pointing towards the boat instead of away from it, this will have the effect of pushing the boat away from the paddle and will move you in a direction away from the paddle side. This stroke is not recommended for general use as it is rather an awkward one to perform. Try it by all means—when the water is warm! As a general rule it is better to perfect draw and sculling draw strokes for both sides of the boat.*)

If you are using a spooned blade, try the concave side facing the boat—it should make the stroke more effective.

(3) *Practice:* Practise the stroke on the opposite side when you can do it well on your 'first' side. Lean out to the stroke: as in the case of the other sideways stroke, it will enable you to reach out further from the boat with the paddle, thus making each stroke more effective and helping the boat in its sideways movement.

Try the sculling draw in different positions in relation to the canoe. In how many directions can you propel the canoe by the use of this stroke? Practise 'emergency situations' where you might have to move the boat sideways in a hurry. Placing of obstacles on still water or the erection of a slalom gate will give you good scope for testing the degree of your proficiency. Note how you can often use a combination of both sideways strokes—draw and sculling draw—to gain the desired movement. Try the 'Wiggle Test'—outlined in Chapter 10.

When you feel proficient in the handling of your canoe you will really begin to feel a part of the boat. You will enjoy feeling it respond to every movement and stroke. The BCU Proficiency Test (see Appendix I) is designed to assess your capabilities, and candidates are required to perform all the

4. On the rocks. The canoeist is leaning the right way (downstream) to avoid a capsize, but he is probably about to hole his boat. If he goes in, he will regret having forgotten his life-jacket!

5. All systems go! A slalom canoeist about to be projected into orbit

skills described in this chapter. Even if you don't feel like actually taking the test, it provides a useful guide to the standard that you should be striving to achieve.

The BCU Advanced Tests are for the experienced canoeist who is competent to demonstrate the more advanced strokes, including the Eskimo Roll. Although it is beyond the scope of this chapter to explain the Advanced strokes it is perhaps worth mentioning, however, that they are simply an extension or mixture of one or more of the basic strokes that have been considered. 'High' strokes, for example, are an adaptation of the basic strokes with the paddle held over the head: a Tele-mark turn combines backward sweep and sculling for support strokes. If the basic strokes are well and truly mastered—and this means practising them to the stage where they come automatically according to the needs of the moment—the canoeist can proceed to study the more advanced strokes with confidence. He is even likely to improvise his own and, indeed, there is a great deal of pleasure to be gained from devising the best possible means of keeping full control over the boat in all kinds of water.

D

3

Inland Touring

KATHLEEN TOOTILL

ONE day just before World War II a little knot of people stood on the shore at Durdle Door in Dorset. The object of their curiosity was a man and wife with a salt-stained, beamy, double canvas canoe. They were touring and they had just rounded Portland Bill. Their aim was to paddle right round Great Britain. More than 100 years ago John (Rob Roy) MacGregor stirred imagination with his long canoe voyages on European rivers. Today probably the majority of canoes are used locally, for day runs, for competition, or for messing about in odd leisure hours. But for those with the urge to rove, the possession of a canoe can mean adventurous travel limited only by the water available.

In these days of specialized canoes, with hulls adapted for straight racing, for slalom, for rivers rapid or slow, or for the sea, the intending tourist will have to decide on a compromise model. His primary need is for adequate space to carry baggage, but he does not want in achieving this to sacrifice all the speed and lightness of the racer, or the manœuvrability of the slalom canoe, for his way may lie along the placid Thames or the turbulent Spey, and in Britain especially with its superb coastline he will surely want to travel on the sea also. A rough guide to this compromise boat that is to be used on all waters not of extreme difficulty suggests a length of 14 ft 6 in. or thereabouts, 24–26-in. beam and a slightly rockered bottom.

Britain, however, may be only part of the picture, for to find rivers long enough for a fortnight's holiday one must go abroad, at least to Europe, and this will suggest the advantages of a folding canoe for both convenience of stowage and cheapness of transport to the chosen river. The intending tourist who is also a specialist need not be debarred from using his specialized canoe, but his racer will deter him from rocky rapids and his well-rockered slalom boat may be slow and tiring on the long flat stretches encountered on most big rivers; wind and waves on slow rivers and canals, and, of course, on sea and estuary, will play havoc with his steering. Double canoes, although proportionately fewer nowadays, crewed by those who know how to work together, can be a joy on wide river and sea and will considerably reduce physical effort. Photographers know the advantage of paddling a double, with one partner controlling the boat while the other presses the trigger; and, of course, with shared camping gear, and the ample stowage space canoe-camping in a double is quite luxurious. But there are excellent and spacious single touring canoes.

The modern tendency is for cockpits to be as small as is compatible with the operation of getting in and out. This means a smaller area of spray cover and a nearer approach to watertightness. But the touring canoeist may prefer a larger cockpit. He is not in a hurry and his object is enjoyment of travel. He wants his equipment to be accessible without having to grope for it, and the larger cockpit facilitates the management of camera, sketching materials, a bird book maybe and a monocular or field glasses, maps and guides, casual food and drink. It is pleasant also to let the sunshine on to one's legs. For the deeper stretches of exposed waters, and for the sea, the double canoe and the long single-seater should have a rudder so that when the wind or waves are on a quarter one can still put equal pressure on either end of the paddle instead of having to overwork one side.

To camp on a canoe tour is not essential: many continental rivers have chains of youth hostels or canoe stations at suitable distances, and in this country some people rely on the village inn. But camping brings freedom of movement and relief from anxiety should the day's programme be interrupted. It is not always possible to judge the distance to be covered in one day, for winds, high or low water, tides, and, of course, the occasional capsize or holed boat, can make a difference sometimes amounting to hours. Again, during the day one may want to linger in some spot or explore awhile on foot, and the knowledge that house and home are stowed below decks makes one carefree. In any case the canoeist who camps experiences pleasure immeasurable: to pitch camp close to the water, boat at hand, to fall asleep to the sound of water, for even the quiet river has its subtle music, to wake next day entranced by those same sounds, mingled with the early calls of birds and water creatures; such things give the canoe-camper full enjoyment. Camping makes possible cruises down the remoter rivers inaccessible to road users and house dwellers.

The intending canoe-camper who has already cycle-camped or pedestrian-camped will have no difficulty in selecting his equipment. The canoe will take rather more bulk and weight than the pedestrian carries on his back, but those who travel light gain greatly when, for instance, portaging round a weir or unshootable fall, when arriving and departing from camp, especially if the bank is steep, and of course when paddling, for a heavily laden boat rides a little lower in the water. Only experience and experiment will provide each canoeist with his ideal camping equipment, but if he thinks in terms of house, bed, kitchen, food, light, clothing, hygiene and hobbies he will have no real difficulty—but the camper who canoes does have a few points to consider beyond those of the plain camper.

House. As the morning pack-up may be wet, a tent with nylon or Terylene flysheet is an advantage, for everything else stays dry and the small wet roll can be stowed separately or can be dried out in a few minutes if the rain stops. A sewn-in groundsheet is invaluable if the river rises unexpectedly in the night and camp has to be shifted, for the whole tent and all in it can be picked up and moved at one go.

Bed. If the sleeping-bag is not quite warm enough, as good as an extra blanket is a long scarf wound round your middle, and this has daytime use as well.

Kitchen. Except in really wild country or below river banks, fires are not often allowed nowadays. The half-pint pressure stove is probably the most convenient and economical cooker for the lightweighter. All food and matches must be in waterproof containers. Polythene bags are good, but these should be kept within tins or some other strong containers. Remember a rat or a cat may drop in for a midnight feast!

Food. Canned food is heavy and bulky; there are so many dehydrated foods available that provisioning is no problem. It is important to think ahead about drinking water and, for safety, carry some on the voyage.

Light. In summer a torch is adequate in Britain. Farther south, or in spring and autumn a supply of candles is useful.

Clothing. Continuous paddling encourages warmth but stopping to eat can be chilling, so several light layers, according to season, are better than one thicker garment, and a light waterproof anorak should be at hand. Some people prefer the freedom of a sou'wester to the anorak hood which may dull the hearing. Plastic sandals, or gym shoes with a few holes to let out the water, are good to wear when canoeing, but for a long stretch in the canoe they can be exchanged for thick woollen socks. Gum boots are bulky and dangerous for a canoeist. A towel, warm jersey and trousers must be carried in case of capsize. In the event of a second capsize there are always one's pyjamas, but there must be no third ducking!

Hygiene. Unless it is known that all camp sites to be used have sanitary arrangements laid on, it is essential for a canoeing party to carry a latrine tent and entrenching tool and to dig only where other tents will not be pitched. For small parties camping only in wild or remote country the minimum necessity is that each person should carry a knife or small trowel and dig for himself. Neglect of this duty may endanger other people's health.

Hobbies. Photographers, sketchers, bird watchers, geologists and writers need not leave their tools at home. Everything that is carried in a canoe should be tied up in a waterproof bag.

Normal buoyancy equipment for a canoe is roughly that of a gallon polythene bottle secured inside each end. With the added weight of camping gear it is advisable to imprison a little air in each of the waterproof bags containing the gear, especially in such things as air pillows. All the gear bags, in addition to being effectively closed, must be tied or securely jammed into the canoe. There are various ways of packing. It is usual to put most of the weight into the ends of the boat, but it should be noted that excessive weight at the ends make the boat less manœuvrable, while much weight amidships, added to that of the paddler, may make the ends swivel too easily. Weight must be distributed so that the canoe rides horizontally. Some people add a long string to packages thrust into the ends, as otherwise they may have to upend the boat to get them out. A package tied to the floor just in front of the seat provides a good relaxing support for the knees. Common sense directs that anything that might be needed during the day, including a canoe repair outfit, should be readily accessible and that the first requisite at the end of the journey, the tent, should be easily at hand. The painter and its fastening must be beyond reproach, for when you make a lunch halt you may not want to lift the laden canoe from the water, and you may have to tie up in a current. If it should be decided to carry the canoe complete with load, it is well to have four carriers, two supporting the cockpit region so as not to strain the shape of the canoe.

Before launching it is most important to remember that canoeing and camping are nowadays activities to which there is a growing opposition that is gradually imposing more and more restrictions. This is partly because of the greatly increased numbers of participants in these wonderful occupations, but it is also the result of inconsiderate behaviour on the part of many of us canoe campers. The future is in our hands. Tidy and quiet camping, leaving no litter and in fact no trace of one's temporary habitation, and a courteous attitude to farmer or landowner, should need no reminder. Before one pitches a tent, permission should be sought. Afloat, it is important to remember that fishermen, like canoeists, should not be interfered with and that not only must their lines be given a wide berth but that if there is any sign that the fisherman is just at a crucial stage of proceedings, the canoeist should wait for a sign to pass and in any case pass if possible with paddles shipped.

Canoeists already experienced in local paddling, and equipped with canoe and camping gear, will take off on experimental tours without difficulty, and after even one weekend will have learnt more than any book could teach. But the inquirer who has not yet tried the game may like to go first on some organized holiday with all equipment provided. The advantage of starting this way is that you are helped to decide whether to commit yourself to the purchase of your own equipment (the answer is seldom in doubt!) and that you build up enough knowledge to enable you to buy or make the right kind of equipment adapted to your own individuality. Several travel organizations—e.g., The Holiday Fellowship, 142 Great North Way, Hendon, London, N.W.4; the Youth Hostels Association, Trevelyan House, St Albans, Herts—include canoe-camping tours in their programmes, but there are also at least two which exist primarily for this kind of holiday—P.G.L. Voyages, The Boathouse, Commerce Lane, Letchworth, Herts, for both British and continental rivers, and Matt Murphy Holiday Enterprises, Ballymaquirk, Banteer, Co. Cork, Eire, chiefly for the river Blackwater. Both these organizations give adventure, good company and good experience. For more formal courses, the Central Council of Physical Recreation, 26–29 Park Crescent, London, W.1 should be approached. Every Easter weekend Britain's largest touring club, The Canoe Camping Club (11 Lower Grosvenor Place, London, S.W.1), holds a meet on some easy but interesting river, often the Wye, Severn, Trent, Thames or Great Ouse, when up to 120 canoe-campers may gather. They come and camp for the four days, tyros and old hands together, young and old, one vast friendly company, and anyone wishing to learn the game could hardly do better than turn up there, even just to be among the vast variety of canoes, tents and gadgets, and mingle with the experience of many waters in many lands. Scouts will already know of the famous Scout cruises run annually by Percy Blandford, who needs no introduction.

But enough of preparation. Let us get afloat and travel. Unless you have already done it with one of the above organizations the Wye is an excellent starter. Do not attempt the rocky upper part but launch at Glasbury. From there to Chepstow are about 100 miles of river without the need for a single portage, easy but with simple manageable rapids occasionally and with the interesting estuarial run on the last day from Tintern to Chepstow when tides must be studied and the run made on the ebb. A special canoeist's map of the Wye is published by P. W. Blandford. For England and Wales in general, get a copy of Stanford's *Canoeing Map of England and Wales*, and for Ireland, *Canoeist's Map of Ireland* (a *Canoeing* publication). Practically the whole of the British Isles is covered in the British Canoe Union's Guide to the Waterways of the British Isles. This, and in fact most of the canoeing maps also, British and foreign, can be bought from BCU Supplies, 26–29 Park Crescent, London, W.1.

When planning your tour you will want to know, how far shall I manage in a day? This is a hard question to answer, for much depends on conditions—speed of water, wind, number of portages, number of hours available for canoeing; whether you like a lazy morning striking camp, enabling the dew to dry off your tent, or an early evening pitching. There is time to be allowed for off-the-river excursions, and there is always the chance of a puncture or a capsize, so a firm estimate is impossible. But *do* start at least one day at dawn! A rough though arbitrary guide to progress is that your pace on a fairly sluggish river may be about that of yourself as pedestrian. For fast rivers add to your speed the speed of the current.

The Severn can be canoed from Llanidloes, but if on a first voyage you want to avoid hazards, start at Welshpool. With the exception of portages at two or three weirs you will have an uninterrupted run of great interest for varied water conditions and scenery as far as Worcester, a distance of just over 100 miles. Below Worcester there is less interest until Gloucester, where the Severn becomes tidal, and these estuarial waters, which provide great variety of experience for the really able canoeist, need most careful study beforehand, particularly because of the exciting bore which at the fortnightly spring tides could be dangerous to the unpractised canoeist.

If further exploration of the quieter rivers is sought, there is the Thames in its gentle and lovely valley—wild river only from Cricklade to Lechlade, thereafter a locked navigation down to Teddington. A licence from the Thames Conservancy is required for this stretch. The voyage can be continued down the tideway to Greenwich or farther if the paddler has some knowledge of tides, estuarial conditions and shipping lanes. The Warwickshire Avon, the Trent, and the Great Ouse are rivers all long enough for a cruise of several days.

For the quiet-water canoeist who likes good scenery, Ireland has much to offer. By canal and the river Shannon it is possible to go from east coast to west (Dublin to Limerick), or to do the length of the Shannon from Lough Allen. Dublin to Waterford is possible by canal and river, while the length of the Blackwater (Cork) makes an ideal cruise comparable in scenery and water to our Wye.

For gradual initiation into rapid river canoeing there is perhaps no finer river than the Scottish Spey, for, from a start at Newtonmore, a couple of days is spent on easy water with shallow rapids of increasing interest, so that by the time one reaches Grantown the heavier and faster water is taken in one's stride, and the little excitement of Knockando rapids lower down can be a highlight of the trip. The Spey, unlike most rivers, has a splendid current right down to the sea.

The newcomer to rapid rivers should remember that guidebook descriptions of rapids and other hazards are usually of what may be called average conditions and that, because they are mountain-fed rivers and have considerable gradient, water levels vary tremendously; whereas after a dry spell much wading

may be necessary, particularly with a loaded boat, flood conditions, which are often sudden, may be difficult and even
unmanageable for those used only to quiet water. However
easy the water is when the day's run begins, precautions must
never be relaxed—all gear must be firmly secured, spray cover
in order and lifejacket worn. Then in the event of a capsize
the day can continue to be one of happy adventure. There was
once a miserable chap who lost everything on the first day of a
fortnight's holiday! It is assumed that no one will venture on a
rapid river without knowing what to do with a canoe caught on
a rock or against the pier of a bridge and in danger of breaking
or of wrapping itself round a tree trunk, though the trained
canoeist should usually be able to avoid getting into such
troubles. Baggage and ropes must be stowed so as not to
entangle the legs, and the spray cover must be self-releasing
from either boat or person, but not from both or it will be lost.

While in Scotland it is certainly worthwhile to cruise down
the Tay from Loch Tay. The voyage can be continued past
Perth down the Firth of Tay to finish at perhaps Dundee or
beyond. On the Tay are many quiet stretches, but the hazards
at Grantully, Campsie Linn (in high water), and Stanley Weir
demand great care. I have seen several canoes wrecked at
Grantully and I personally find it comforting first to unload
my camping gear on to the bank a little way above, afterwards
retrieving it by walking back and re-stowing it in the calm water
well below the bridge. Again, while in Scotland, if there is time,
make that rewarding trip through the Walter Scott country
down the Tweed, launching perhaps at Peebles. The Tweed
has some exciting rapids and shootable caulds (weirs) and it is
advisable to stop and prospect some of them, notably the ones
at Makerston, before committing oneself with a loaded canoe.

Apart from these rivers of considerable volume it should be
borne in mind that most of Britain's rapid rivers, except after
a distinctly rainy period, may offer a number of rocky rapids
too shallow for a laden touring canoe, and whereas wading and
towing for occasional short distances may be a pleasant game,
too much of it is wearying, and the extra inches below waterline of a laden boat may cause a deal of wading unnecessary
with an empty canoe. An exception among rapid rivers is the
Welsh Teifi which, being fed from marshy uplands, is rarely
very low and provides a delightful and exciting run from
Tregaron down to the sea.

Every year great numbers of canoe-campers plan to do their touring abroad. In addition to the natural desire to see more of the world there is the lure of bigger and more exciting rivers and the knowledge that there will be no question of trespass. In England at the time of writing the right of canoeists to use any but the few public navigations is being challenged. The difficulty is that a river has not one owner but many—in fact, as many as there are owners of stretches of the banks. To make a legal voyage it may be necessary to ask and receive permission from them all. It has been known for eleven owners to say yes, while the twelfth said, no. The reason for this difficulty is considered to be the enormous increase in both canoeists and fishermen. On some rivers, used by canoeists for years, there are now notices forbidding canoeing. Little wonder then that we are abandoning home waters for the more friendly foreign river life.

So let us see what Europe has to offer. Those who prefer to start their continental canoeing with a group can, as for the Wye at home, join one of the organizations mentioned above and tour with all equipment provided, largely on popular rivers such as the Rhône, Rhine, Mosel and Danube. The BCU has made arrangements to take parties by coach with a trailer equipped to carry the canoes, for tours of French and German and possibly other rivers. Members of these parties will have their own equipment. Outside these organizations there is the choice of using public transport or taking one's own car to reach the river. If there is but one car in the party and no non-canoeing driver, the car will be abandoned at the start of the voyage and there is the matter of getting back to it. But river valleys are often bus and train routes, so the driver can usually find some way of getting back to his car. When a party has two or more cars a popular, though time-consuming, method is for at least two cars to be taken to the proposed end of the voyage and one of them to return to the start carrying both or all the drivers. Then when the voyage is ended there will be at least one waiting car, which will immediately convey back the other drivers so as to bring all cars to the end to be loaded. The advantage of using public transport is the avoidance of all this car shuttling, which few people really enjoy. Continental trains are accustomed to carrying rigid canoes, but buses can manage only folding ones. The Touring Club de France, 62 Avenue Parmentier, Paris 11e, has done a great deal for canoeing, producing specialized maps and guides. In that country there are rivers to suit every taste although, as almost everywhere else nowadays, hydro-electric barrages are becoming more numerous spoiling long stretches of water for the canoeist and necessitating often laborious portages. For this reason an essential part of one's equipment, unless it is known that there will be no long portages, is a small folding trolley carried in the canoe or strapped on the deck.

For a start in France, try the river with the most magnificent, even startling scenery, the Ardeche. It rises in the Cevennes country, scene of R. L. Stevenson's travels with Modestine, and winds eastwards through a stupendous gorge to join the Rhône near Pont St Esprit The wonderful thing about this river is that, running in places between enormous vertical cliffs where one might expect unshootable torrents, it is actually easy enough for a beginner and its sparkling little rapids need cause no alarm in summer time except after a phenomenal storm; in this case even camping is dangerous, for the river rises at an incredible pace, and from a camp on a ledge in the gorge, a favourite place, there would be no escape except by water. On one memorable occasion, reading the portents, we put a canoe by each tent, then about midnight, when the flood came, each tent was moved intact with contents and bundled into a canoe. Luckily, on this occasion there was a higher terrace to which it was possible to carry everything. Paddling through the main gorge takes two to three days and in this part there is no road access as yet. The lightest camp equipment is all that is needed and it is quite usual not to bother to pitch tent but to lie out on the flat sunbaked slabs of rock. A store of local grapes and peaches, a yard or two of French bread, will stave off the wolf, but it is as well to take a large water-carrier, for drinking water is obtainable at only two springs in the gorge. The river is literally thick with fish. At one point it is bridged by a natural arch, the Pont d'Arc, where the water has cut through a limestone cliff and the prehistoric ox bow now dry can be viewed from the cliff top. Naturally, a superb journey like this is popular, and dozens of canoes of many nationalities pass down the gorge every day. That adds to the interest, and by the time you have exchanged ideas with these many new friends you will have no need of further advice on continental rivers from books for you will get it first hand. If you do not capsize accidentally on the Ardeche, you will probably do it on purpose—for the delicious cooling swim. Lower down the Rhône, on the left bank, comes in the Durance. This is a river very different from the Ardeche. Rising in the Alpes Hautes near Briançon and the Italian border, its milky glacial waters rush down an Alpine valley, in places at a good gradient, giving quite formidable rapids. Rapid river experience is desirable before an attempt is made on this river, and capsize drill should be familiar, for immersion in these icy waters could be harmful, even lethal. About 35 km. down from l'Argentière, a good starting point, the river wells up into a huge reservoir entailing a 12 km. portage, but it is well worth starting again below down the still exciting current and continuing to the Rhône junction, though the last day's journey is on slow water. The Rhône itself used to provide an excellent longish cruise from near the Swiss border to the Mediterranean, but in recent years several barrages have been built, necessitating lengthy portages and making the water more sluggish. These French examples are only a few. There are other good rivers joining the Rhône, and farther west those of the Gironde basin, for example the Tarn, Dordogne, Lot and the pleasant but less exciting rivers that join the Loire, are worth consideration. Take a good map of France, plan your tour, then write to the T.C.F. for advice and details of your proposed rivers.

Germany, Austria, northern Italy, Yugoslavia, Poland, Spain, Sweden, to mention only a few, have a wealth of canoeable rivers, and all have organizations which will help the British canoeist. A list is given in Appendix II. These countries have their rivers graded according to an international code and this will help your selection. Several countries organize international canoe touring events at which you will be welcomed. For example, in Austria one can go to a base camp on the Chiem See, whence coach parties are taken daily under leaders to launching spots on rivers of various grading, so that one can progress daily to more advanced paddling.

Perhaps you are more adventurous than to want merely to join other canoeists or even to paddle the well-known rivers. Does the unknown attract you? I have been lucky on several occasions in finding companions who were keen to pioneer new routes for canoeists. In 1952 we were probably the firs west European canoeists to paddle the Yugoslavian Drian In 1957 we went to find the possibilities of Iceland and had thrilling voyages down the Hvita, the Thegandi and the Blanda. We found many rivers which will provide first-class experience for future canoeists once they can overcome travel difficulties in a land so lacking in roads that ponies and planes are the most usual way of getting about. Bulgaria in 1963 was another venture into a land where canoeing had been limited to a large reservoir made by the Stalin dam on the river Iskar near Sofia. There we had a wildly exciting run down the Rilske and the Struma and a quieter but more beautiful run along the Kamchiya and into the Black Sea. At that time wild camping was illegal but we willingly endured three hours' arrest for the privilege! The long river Maritza, not fully explored by us, suggests an admirable canoe-camping journey.

Although most European countries now have their canoe organizations and there are not, therefore, many still unvisited by Britons, there remain, for those with the initiative to seek them out, many remote rivers, on which canoe has not yet floated. Europe is of course not the limit. Canoeists in Australia, New Zealand, Canada, the USA, Africa and South America have already blazed trails for you, while countless waters through lands exciting beyond our wildest dreams may one day be paddled by the young and adventurous of many countries.

4

Coastal Touring

NORMAN SUDRON

COASTAL touring by canoe has thrills and challenges to offer which demand from its followers a high degree of physical fitness together with a sound knowledge of canoeing technique and sea-lore.

This chapter is directed at the canoeist who, having mastered his craft on calm and sheltered waters, now wishes to go further afield.

I feel I must stress before I begin that the canoeing novice should not attempt coastal touring until he is a strong and confident swimmer, and, to quote the BCU Sea Proficiency Test, 'he is a strong paddler against adverse conditions of wind and tide'. And even then only in the company of experienced canoeists.

CANOES FOR COASTAL TRIPS

The type of canoe used for coastal work should have certain essential features. These are as follows:

(*a*) A length not less than 15 feet on the waterline. Length and a straight keel make it easier to paddle a straight course, particularly when the wind and waves are on the beam or aft.

(*b*) Strong construction, with all materials of top quality and in good condition.

(*c*) A foot-operated rudder; this also helps to maintain course.

(*d*) Ample stowage space for buoyancy and kit without encroaching on cockpit space.

Whether the coastal tourist uses a single or a double canoe for his trips is a matter of personal preference, but I must admit to an opinion that the double canoe is safer for sea tours and, I feel, is more stable in rough water. Its principal advantage, however, lies in being 'twin-engined', which is good for morale in a tricky situation. In addition to this, one of the crew can take bearings or stoke up with food while the other keeps way on the canoe.

SEA EQUIPMENT

For the Canoe
COLOURS: Bright colours show up well on the sea, orange or yellow standing out best. Remember, a canoe is a tiny craft on the sea and is not easily spotted at the best of times.
SPRAY COVER: This is essential and should be tailored to the canoe. It must keep out not only spray, but also heavy waves which may be thrown over the canoe. At the same time it must be instantly detachable in an emergency.
BUOYANCY: Ample buoyancy should always be carried and securely fixed in the bow and stern of the canoe.
PAINTER: At least 20 feet of thin line should be attached to rings at the bow and stern and taken to cleats at the side of the cockpit.
PADDLES: A spare should be carried in two parts, securely fastened to the deck and accessible from the cockpit.
REPAIR KIT: A kit suitable for the type of construction used in the canoe should be included in the equipment carried.
BALER: A plastic baler will prove useful, and, with a sponge, will keep the craft dry.
COMPASS: An essential piece of equipment; more of this later in the chapter.
FLARES: Sometimes expensive, but for sea tours an essential investment. Usually supplied in waterproof packing, and can be stored in the cockpit where they are easily reached.

For the Canoeist
CLOTHING: The usual type of canoeing clothing, with a good anorak to keep out spray. In cold weather a slalom jacket might prove beneficial, but perhaps too warm for long periods of paddling.
LIFE-JACKETS: These are of course a 'must' for any canoeist. They should be worn and not merely carried in the cockpit. Don't be pennywise; buy a good quality one from a reputable manufacturer. A 'buoyancy aid' is not enough. Invest in the

life-jacket recommended by the BCU and advertised in all canoeing magazines.

WHISTLE: Preferably made of plastic. Useful for signalling. Attach to the life-jacket by a lanyard.

WRISTWATCH: A waterproof one should be carried by at least one of the group. Useful for timing progress and run of the tide, etc.

RADIO: A small transistor set wrapped in a plastic bag can be used for obtaining weather forecasts *en route*.

STOWAGE OF GEAR

Bulky gear such as camping kit, bedding, clothes, etc., should never be carried in the cockpit; in a capsize it could trap the canoeists's legs. Stow this kit in heavy-gauge plastic bags, folding the neck over three or four times. Now place each bag in a waterproof canvas kitbag, fold the neck of this and tie securely. In a capsize, gear packed like this will give extra buoyancy, and will remain dry. These bags must be stowed under the decking, heavy kit aft to trim the canoe slightly by the stern, and tied in to prevent loss in a capsize. Food will keep dry in the air-tight plastic containers now on the market. Screw-top jars are useful for sugar, tea, etc.

On a long haul it pays to have 'energy' foods in a convenient place in the cockpit. Chocolate, dried fruit, barley sugar, nuts, etc., together with a glucose drink or hot drink of tea or soup in a flask. It is amazing how a quick snack at frequent intervals wards off fatigue.

THE COMPASS

Whilst we cannot liken our short coastal trips to an Atlantic crossing, and the prudent canoeist will be a 'coast hugger', it is essential that he has a working knowledge of the use of the compass as well as how to plot his position by a 'fix' and how to use a chart.

The compass used by the coastal canoeist must be reliable and of necessity the hand-held type. The following features should be looked for when choosing it.

COASTAL TOURING   65

(a) Liquid damped for steady readings.

(b) Eye-level sighting prism for taking bearings when afloat.

(c) Graduated external ring which can be locked on a bearing.

(d) Reasonably light in weight for ease in taking bearings when handheld.

A compass which fulfils all the above requirements and can be recommended for coastal work, is the Army-type prismatic compass which is available in most surplus stores for £3 or £4. The canoeist cannot expect to navigate with the accuracy of the skilled yachtsman because of the low freeboard and the diminutive size of his craft compared with even the smallest cruising yacht, but with a good compass and chart, and with practice, he will help to ensure his safety on the sea.

Use of the Compass

In the marine compass there is a rotating circle of card known as the compass rose. Set in the card are a number of small magnets which cause the card to swing and indicate the Magnetic North. The card is calibrated in degrees, North is 0 degrees, East is 90 degrees, South is 180 degrees, West is 270 degrees, and round to 360 degrees brings us back to North. It is important to realize that there is a difference between Geographical or True North, and Magnetic North; this difference is known as the 'magnetic variation', and in Britain varies between $9\frac{1}{2}$ degrees and 15 degrees west of True North, depending on which part of the British Isles one is in.

The coastal chart has on it a compass rose showing Magnetic North, and bearings may be taken direct from it. A check should be made, however, that the north given is Magnetic North. If, as sometimes happens, the type of chart being used gives a Truth North compass rose, allowance must be made for the magnetic variation which will be given on the chart. The corrected bearing will then be your magnetic bearing by which all courses are steered.

TAKING A DIRECT BEARING

To take a direct bearing on an object, the compass is held steadily in the hand and sighted on the object. A glance through the prism will give the bearing of the object off the compass card.

E

CHART BEARINGS

To take a bearing off a chart, lay the chart flat and place the compass in the centre of the compass rose of the chart. Now rotate the chart until the North/South hairline on the compass coincides with the magnetic north on the chart. A line drawn from the object to the centre of the compass rose will enable the bearing to be read off. The canoeist preparing for a coastal trip will need to take several of these bearings as will be explained later. Practice in taking bearings, both direct on landmarks and also from charts or Ordnance Survey maps, should be indulged in frequently until the canoeist is able to take them quickly and accurately.

CHARTS

The best kind of charts to use are large-scale coastal charts because the distances covered in the 'legs' of a coastal tour are usually only a few miles. The Admiralty charts are the most complete, and an annual catalogue is published giving the latest details of the range available. They are, however, rather large, and not very handy to use in a canoe. If a more handy size is required, the 'Stanford' range can be recommended. They are in colour, and give a wealth of information. It is possible to use the large-scale Ordnance Survey maps for planning coast trips, but as they do not give the information about tidal streams and currents found on the coastal charts, they should only be used when knowledge of the local conditions can be obtained in other ways, best of all from the fishermen if this is possible.

Charts can be obtained from most marine stockists or ordered through any bookseller. They are somewhat expensive, but worth buying if a lot of coastal work is envisaged. Anyone can soon become quite proficient at chart reading as the charts are largely self-explanatory.

To sum up:

(a) Buy a good-quality chart.

(b) Learn to read it easily and quickly until a glance at it gives you a clear mental picture of the area it covers.

(c) Practise using it as much as you can, even on trips when you do not really require it.

TAKING A 'FIX'

Finding your position, or taking a 'fix', as it is called, requires the use of a chart and a compass. There are several methods of doing this, but we will only concern ourselves with two main ones.

The Single Bearing

With a compass, a bearing is taken on a prominent object such as a headland, lighthouse, radio mast, church, etc., and the distance the landmark is from your position is estimated. The position of your craft can now be plotted on the chart. As distances are not easy to estimate with any degree of accuracy, this method is only a rough guide, but may be the only choice if mist or thick weather give nothing more than an occasional glimpse of a landmark, when a quick bearing must be taken and a course set to give a landfall.

The Cross Bearing

For this method, two landmarks are required, and they should be at about 90 degrees to each other. A bearing is taken on each object, and these are transferred to the chart. Where the bearings intersect, this is your position.

TIDES

The tides and their movements are an important factor to be considered by the canoeist. The length of time from High Water to the next High Water is about 12 hours. The tides vary in the amount by which they rise and fall. There are two types of tide to consider—the spring-tide and the neap-tide.

Spring-tides: This is the period when the range of tidal rise and fall is at its greatest, and during the springs the coastal streams and currents travel at their fastest, influenced also by weather conditions.

Neap-tides: These are the opposite to the springs, and during the neap period the rise and fall of the tide has its smallest range, and the tidal streams slacken off their rate.

You will find on the marine chart in the reference to tides a chart Tide Datum Level. This datum level is the level of the average low-water spring-tide. The chart will tell you the amount by which the spring- and neap-tides will exceed the chart datum at various harbours on the chart, and it will also tell you the speed and direction of the local tidal currents.

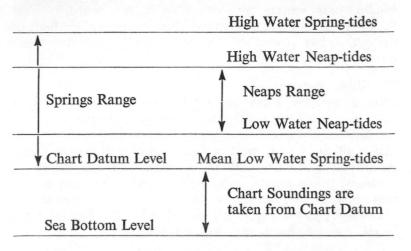

Tide Tables: These are obtained from any fishing tackle stockist and yacht chandler, and are an essential part of the sea canoeist's equipment. Using the tables, one can calculate the times and directions of the tides on the part of the coast which is to be explored. It can be seen from the tables whether the tides are spring or neap or in between because the heights of the tides at high and low water are given for the area in which the tables are published. Full information for the nearest main port is given, together with brief details for other ports and harbours in the area. Tides are, of course, affected by weather conditions. For instance, a spring-tide which is backed up by a very strong wind will rise above the level given in the tide tables. Conversely, if the tide is opposed by a wind, the level will be less than that given in the tables. All these factors must be taken into account when planning a tour.

Tidal Streams
Before starting out to make a coastal passage it is important to plan your course carefully in order to make as much use as possible of the flow of the tide. The 'legs' of the course should be covered if possible running with the tidal stream. Better progress is likely to be made with the tide in one's favour than with the wind in one's favour and an adverse tidal stream, although this will of course depend on the relative strengths of

the wind and the tide. The direction and speed of currents are governed by the type of coastline, and reference must be made to the chart in order to choose a safe course and avoid potentially dangerous ones. As a general rule the canoeist will stay as close to the shore as possible, but he must be prepared to make detours to avoid dangerous areas. In the open sea the tidal stream is at its slowest, whilst in narrow channels and around headlands it speeds up considerably.

Headlands
These almost always create a fast current or race which takes a seaward direction before sweeping back in a circle. If a shelf of rock is present off the headland it will cause an 'overfall', which can be recognized by broken water and should be avoided by the canoeist. Between the overfall or race and the headland there may be a channel of smooth water, but this may be very dangerous. It is invariably safer to give every overfall or race a very wide berth indeed.

Reefs
As a general rule it is safer for the canoeist to avoid these as much as possible because the currents round them are unpredictable. They will show up as broken water when covered. If the chart shows them to be well covered at high water, then at such times they may be safely crossed.

Shallows
When shallows extend out to sea for a considerable distance they will cause a heavy swell in the area and heavy surf on the shore, especially after storms further out at sea. The swell is safe to negotiate, but keep well clear of any surf, and any area where the swell is starting to 'lip' over.

River Mouths and Estuaries
In these areas care should be exercised because tidal races are produced, and where tidal streams meet there may be much broken and confused water. Areas, too, where fresh water meets salt water are potentially dangerous because the fresh water sinks below the salt water and down currents are created.

Rip-tides
Where any open beach is pounded by surf a considerable

pressure of water is built up. This pressure is relieved by out-going currents known as 'rip-tides'. These currents can travel at a fair speed and every year are responsible for the deaths of swimmers caught in them and carried out to sea. The natural reaction of a swimmer caught in one and finding that he is being swept out to sea is to turn and swim furiously for the shore. No progress is made against the force of the current, the swimmer soon tires, and is then swept away and drowned. If the swimmer can force himself to do the unnatural thing and allow himself to be carried out by the rip until the current slackens off, he will then be able to swim along the back of the breakers and come in on the incoming waves.

To sum up: Study your chart well, pick your course with care, avoid obvious dangers, and keep a weather eye open for the not so obvious ones. Treat all patches of broken water with extreme caution, and know your local tides and currents.

It should be noted that the safest time to navigate areas where currents are known to exist is one hour before or after the times of high and low water. At those times currents are running at their slackest.

WEATHER FORECASTING

It is essential that the coastal canoeist should have some knowledge of the basis of weather forecasting. Making use of natural signs it is possible to form some idea of the type of weather which will be encountered during a trip. The following remarks are offered as a guide, and a much fuller study of weather reading may be made by reading one of the many books on the subject. It is strongly emphasized, however, that the proper course of action is to consult the nearest meteorological office by telephone immediately before setting off.

Clouds
The type of sky observed and the clouds it contains are a good basic guide. There are four main types of cloud formation with which we will concern ourselves.

CUMULUS: A medium altitude cloud of lumpy appearance usually towering up. Common during thunderstorms.

NIMBO-STRATUS: A heavy dark-coloured cloud which forms at low altitude. A rain bearing cloud.

CIRRUS: A feathery cloud at high altitude gives the 'mackerel sky' effect seen in fine weather.

STRATUS: A layer of cloud similar to fog. When the word stratus is used with the names of other clouds it means those clouds have formed in layers, e.g., strato-cumulus means a layer of cumulus clouds.

Barometric Pressure

The height of the barometer gives an indication of the weather. A high barometer reading means dry and fine weather, a low reading wet and stormy weather. When the barometer starts to rise, fine weather is on the way, when it falls, bad weather is due.

The effect of barometric pressure on tidal level is also important. Barometric pressure acts as an inverted barometer. High pressure will lower sea level, while low pressure will raise it by 1 foot for a pressure fall of 34 mbs. Surges of pressure may raise the sea level by many feet; e.g., at Harwich in 1953, when predicted high water level was 5·5 feet and actual height was 12·2 feet, rising subsequently to 13·1 feet—this was the effect of a surge in the North Sea.

ANTI-CYCLONE: An area of high pressure with stability the dominant feature. In winter clear skies give warm days and cold nights with virtually no wind. Cloudy skies give what is termed 'anti-cyclone gloom', and it never becomes really bright. Winds are slight. There is no rain though mist or fog are very common. In summer clear skies give hot days though often relatively cool evenings. Winds are light. Visibility depends on the air mass over the area. If it is a northerly air mass it will give good visibility with NNW winds. Winds from the south give much poorer visibility due to the higher humidity.

DEPRESSIONS: An area of low atmospheric pressure with the pressure rising towards the edge of the depression and accompanied by anti-cyclonic winds. It consists of two different air masses, a cold and a warm one, which are moving along two lines or fronts. The warm front approaches first, being associated with increasing cloud and then fairly steady rain lasting for some four hours—'rain by seven, fine by eleven'. When this front has passed, the humidity rises markedly and visibility is poor—this is the area of warm air known as the warm sector. The advancing cold front brings heavy, sharp showers, often with squally conditions and a marked drop in temperature.

Pressure drops as the depression approaches, levels out in the warm sector and then rises as the cold front goes through. Cirrus giving the 'mackerel sky' effect appear in fine weather, but if they start to form a layer which gradually drops in altitude, then take care, for bad weather is on the way.

The Sky

The appearance of the sky at sunset and at dawn is often a guide to what type of weather can be expected during the day. The rhyme

'A red sky at night, Shepherd's delight,

Red sky at morning, Shepherd's warning.'

is quite a reliable one.

A pale blue sky with red tints and soft woolly clouds at sunset is usually the herald of a fine day. If the sky at sunset is pale yellow or grey with more dense clouds, then this is usually a sign of rain and wind to follow.

At dawn a grey or blue sky containing fleecy clouds foretells fine weather to come, but if the sky is dark blue and clear at dawn, then the prospects are wind and rain.

When at sea on a fine day with a fairly fresh breeze coming from seaward, if the weather appears unsettled, then it pays to keep an eye on the horizon. A rain squall will be seen as a misty patch out at sea, and if such a patch (there may be more than one) is spotted, then the canoeist should make for shelter. When such a squall arrives there will be a large increase in the force of the wind, which may appear to blow from several directions, and there will be driving rain.

Animal Signs

Another quite reliable guide is the behaviour of sea birds. Often before the approach of a storm seagulls will circle at high altitude, or will form up and fly inland. Flocks of gulls out at sea indicate a spell of fine weather. Shoals of fish such as mackerel or herring, or even jellyfish, will be seen near the surface during settled weather.

RULES OF THE ROAD

Most of these apply only to larger craft, but it is quite important that the sea canoeist has a knowledge of the more common ones. This knowledge will be of special value to those canoeists who do most of their canoeing in the vicinity of ports used by shipping. Adherence to the rules will do a lot to improve relations between the port authorities who use the waters for their livelihood, and the canoeists who use them for sport. There is unfortunately no doubt that in some ports these relations are regrettably poor. The approaches to a large port are usually marked by means of deep, dredged lanes called 'Fairways'. The fairway is usually marked by buoys.

It is important that canoeists keep to the side of these fairways or clear of them completely if possible. When proceeding along a fairway, remember the rule of the road at sea is KEEP TO THE RIGHT. When entering a fairway or estuary it will be seen that all the buoys on the starboard side are conical in shape, whilst on the port side the buoys are cylindrical or can-shaped.

The starboard conical buoys are painted all black or black-and-white checks, and the port can buoys are red or red-and-white checks.

Sandbanks or the middle ground are usually marked by spherical buoys painted in horizontal bands of red and white.

Deep water in the middle of the main channel is marked by buoys of varying shapes, other than can- or conical-shaped, painted in vertical stripes of red and white, or black and white.

Wrecks are indicated by green buoys with the word WRECK in white on the side. They may be can or conical buoys indicating on which side it is safe to pass, or spherical if they may be passed on either side. Safe channels are sometimes marked by bell buoys.

The canoeist entering a river mouth should exercise caution when crossing the 'bar', the term given to the place in the river mouth where a sandbank is usually formed at the side of the dredged channel. This bar can be nasty when a swiftly flowing tide which is opposed by a strong wind causes a heavy breaking swell on the bar itself.

In the fairway, as stressed before, keep to the right and out of the way of shipping. After all, 10,000-ton cargo ships are not fitted with disc brakes, and fairways do not allow large ships room for violent evasive action to miss canoeists cutting across their bows. It is not fair to give a pilot or skipper the choice of running you down or putting his ship aground. Large vessels which are deeply laden, such as tankers, cause a heavy wash, so be prepared to turn to meet the wash bows on as the vessel passes. Tugboats in particular cause a nasty wash, although on my own river, the Tees, the tugs slow right down when they sight anyone canoeing in the area.

Keep clear also of dredging operations and boats using divers. Do not moor your canoe, unless in an emergency, to any buoy, light tower, navigation aid, barge platform or jetty reserved for official use. Please also respect fishermens' marking buoys, crab-pots and nets. Canoeing in estuaries and rivers demands only that you follow the rules outlined above and use common sense during your wanderings.

PLANNING THE TOUR

We come now to the day when we desire to put our knowledge to the test and make our first coastal trip of reasonable distance, first having made several day trips along different portions of the nearest coastline. The distance we plan for will depend on several factors:

(a) The number of days we plan to spend on the tour

(b) The type of canoe we are going to use

(c) The degree of fitness of the party.

As a general rule it will be wise to allow a daily run of fifteen to twenty miles. The distance can of course be adjusted to suit the needs of the party. It is worth mentioning at the beginning that the party should be made up of not less than three canoes, whether singles or doubles are to be used.

The next item to be decided is the starting point of the tour and how the party, its equipment, canoes, etc. are all to be transported to this point. The probable finishing point and transport back from it should also be considered.

We must now make sure we have a large-scale chart or charts of the area together with our tide tables. The chart should be studied as often as possible by all members of the party until every detail of the coast has been assimilated.

The canoes themselves should be thoroughly checked over and any necessary work on them completed.

When all the items of kit to be taken on the tour have been assembled, the canoes should be loaded on land with the kit, and adjustments made until the best method of stowing each item has been found. Items required last should of course be stowed first, remembering that if the tents are placed in the canoe last, this will be a boon if it should happen to be raining when a

landing is made, and putting up the tents will be the first task.
Having completed these preparations, we must now plan the
course to be followed. The camp-sites should be selected and, if
possible, visited by road beforehand in order that, where
necessary, permission to camp may be obtained. Also on the
chart we should select a number of spots where an easy landing
can be made in an emergency. Sheltered bays with a good beach,
small fishing ports, etc., will serve as our emergency landing
grounds.

The positions of prominent landmarks such as lighthouses
(together with the type of flashing signals they emit), radio
masts, churches, hills, headlands, etc., should be carefully noted
for future reference.

The times and directions of the tides should be calculated in
order that full advantage may be taken of their help by arranging our travelling to suit as far as possible the run of the tidal
stream.

A weather forecast to cover the period of the tour for the area
in which we plan to canoe can be obtained from the Meteorological Office in London for a nominal fee. Another 'must'
before starting is to pay a visit to the Coastguard Station near
your starting point and inform them of your intentions, giving
them such details as starting time, camping places, the 'leg' you
hope to cover each day, number of canoes in the party, duration
of tour, etc. If you do this, you will be closely watched all the
way along the coast, and handed from station to station. This
is a very comforting thought, especially if the weather begins to
change for the worse.

In the event of a sudden change for the worse in weather
conditions, do not attempt to be the hardy seafarer, paddling
doggedly on with stiff upper lip, otherwise you could end up
being stiff all over. Be a coward. After all, you have no audience
on the sea! Check your position and make for your nearest
emergency landing area. It is far better to land in plenty of time
before the storm, even if it should prove to be a false alarm, than
end up in dire trouble because you thought those famous last
words: 'We should be able to get to our next camp site before
those black clouds over there reach us.' Having fled ignomini-
ously from a few storms, I have always been astounded by the
phenomenal speed with which they can overhaul a fleeing
canoeist. In unsettled weather, always stay close inshore, even
if it means more miles to paddle, and a new camp-site to arrange

at the end of it; after all, you can always sleep on the beach. As an extra safeguard, it is worthwhile to take a few bearings off the chart when you are planning the tour. Use any headland or small island as your bearing point and from it take bearings in different directions to be noted down and used if needed. Most coastal work is visual, but I do remember one occasion when we were caught by a sea mist which came down in minutes, completely obscuring the land and most parts of the sea. One of my companions had wisely taken a compass bearing of our destination before the mist hid it. The distance was about 5 miles, and, despite a cross current, we arrived right on our estimated landing place. The moral to this is: 'Take care, take bearings, and trust your compass.'

5

Canoe Surfing and the Eskimo Roll[1]

DAVID SUTCLIFFE

BOARD surfing is already an immensely popular sport in Cornwall, but canoeists who can roll have a unique opportunity of
acquiring surf skills quickly because they are up and off again
at once after a spill, or 'wipe-out'. Canoe surfing is a new,
dramatic and exciting facet of sea canoeing. Eskimo kayaks are
the ideal craft for the big waves well off-shore, but do not
compare with the modern slalom boats for intensive manœvr-
ability in the breaking water. For strength and reduction of
maintenance problems, glass-fibre boats are much to be
preferred. But too much rocker or curve on the keel line is a
disadvantage because it makes the canoe swing violently,
particularly at the critical moment of accelerating into the
planing position down the wave.

Waves begin to 'feel' the bottom when the depth of water is
half the distance between the wave crests. Once a wave has
begun to feel the bottom its characteristics change, and one
result is a swinging around of direction until the wave front is
parallel to the shore. Good surfing waves require deep water
close to the coast and, for the last mile or two, a gently shelving
bottom. If the beach is too steep one gets 'dumpers'. By far
the best beaches in the country for surfing are those in North
Cornwall facing the Atlantic swell, but most sandy, gently
shelving beaches will offer good surfing conditions at times,
though not with regularity.

Canoe surfing has its own hazards, and safety precautions
must be rigorously observed. Rocks and stones are dangerous.
Rip currents (outgoing currents caused on a rising tide by the

[1] A great deal of the material in this chapter on rolling and canoe surfing
has been taken from writings on the subject by Rear-Admiral D. J.
Hoare, notably the drawings illustrating the principle of the Eskimo Roll,
and the specimen lesson of instruction.
NOTE: Also see photographs between pages 176 and 177.

pressure of the incoming water) need not be dangerous but should be known about. An observer should be stationed if possible above beach level and equipped with binoculars to give warning of any canoeist in trouble after a capsize. A simple set of signals (come in, go further out, left, right, help required, bring help in this/that direction) must be agreed on. It is sensible to keep one or two people on the water's edge, not in canoes, ready to assist others coming ashore, perhaps swimming with a waterlogged canoe. It goes without saying that in heavy surf every canoeist should be a reliable roller and a confident swimmer, and that the canoe must have good buoyancy. But by far the greatest hazard is that of ramming a fellow canoeist or a swimmer. Some local Councils have very sensibly prohibited canoe surfing on their beaches during the summer months because of the bathers. Purchase or construction of a neoprene wetsuit, and a decision to surf in the winter, when conditions are much more exciting anyway, is the best reaction to these Council decisions. If bathing and canoe surfing take place simultaneously on the same beach, separate areas must be marked off with flags.

Collision between canoeists, which can be just as, if not more, serious, can only be avoided by common sense and consideration for others. Do not allow too many surfers in too small an area. Do not paddle in front of someone bearing down on you or about to take off on a wave. Do not take off on a wave until you see a clear run in front of you. If a collision threatens, CAPSIZE—if you are about to hit someone, the drag of your body will halt your canoe at once, or at worst swing it sideways if you are in the crest of a breaking wave; if you are about to be hit, your canoe will take the blow instead of you. Wear a crash helmet as well as a life jacket. Fix soft bumpers to the bow and stern of your canoe (best constructed with neoprene rubber and Evostik), and make others do the same.

These safety precautions may appear severe, but within a few hours of starting a newcomer to surfing may be moving at 20 knots over the ground in a solid object weighing 45 lb., with no directional control and probably not even able to see where he is going. A collision under these circumstances must be serious and could even be fatal.

Learning to handle a canoe in surf is best done in certain well-defined stages.

STABILITY IN BROKEN WATER

1. Paddle out thirty or forty yards. Turn sideways to the breaking waves. Place the paddle over the incoming waves as an outrigger, blade flat on the surface, and allow yourself to be carried ashore. Do this on both sides. Practise moving from the low to the high telemark position and back again as you are carried in. (If instructing, insist that the pupil remains within the white water area—all learners prefer to face the waves and therefore paddle too far out, thus wasting their time. Insist on repetition until the pupil can take a wave breaking on him at shoulder height with confidence—until he is looking around him and moving the boat on his hips instead of staring fixedly at the oncoming water. Be ready to pick him up after a capsize to save time wasted on emptying out.)

2. Position yourself as before. As you rush sideways, lean backwards and sweep the paddle to the stern to act as a rudder. The canoe will run forward. Lean forward the next time, and bring the paddle forward. The canoe will turn to run backwards, but a quick steadying stroke is needed on the other side. Leaning well into the wave is vital. Practise on both sides.

3. Now try running in with small waves. Paddle firmly well before the wave arrives. The canoe will swing sideways very quickly. Capsizes will be frequent until you have learnt to swing your weight and your paddle into the wave as the boat turns.

4. Improve your balance by surfing backwards. The canoe swings sideways much more violently. A high telemark and pronounced shift in weight are necessary.

5. Practise breaking out of a wave from the sideways position by leaning well forward, moving from a high telemark to a draw stroke and, if necessary, adding a few, quick, forward strokes on both sides as the canoe swings to face the waves.

6. Surf in sideways with the paddle above your head, relying on balance alone for stability.

Progress up to this stage will have been possible, though frequently frustrated, without the Eskimo roll. But now, if you cannot roll, go away and learn. If you can, build up your expertise with the following:—

(i) Positioned broadside to the waves, capsize shorewards as a big one arrives and roll up into it.

(ii) Holding the paddle in the Pawlata starting position, capsize as before and experience the sensation of being rolled over several times by the same wave as the white water grips your carefully placed paddle blade.

(iii) Practise capsizing and waiting for one, two, three waves to break over you before rolling up again. This underwater conditioning is important if you are to tackle big surf with confidence and safety.

Let us now move out to the green waves beyond the line of breaking surf. The first skill to acquire here is effective use of the stern rudder stroke, using the paddle blade trailing aft to steer the boat. This skill is harder to acquire, and has a far greater potential for excitement, than would appear at first sight, but it is essential for manœuvrability on the slopes of green waves. Lean freely into the paddle as you apply stern rudder. The real potential of this skill is felt when, as you are running left across the face of a large wave, you apply stern rudder on the right-hand side, lean hard to the right (and downhill!) and, with a thrilling burst of acceleration and in a flurry of spray, swing back down into the trough in front of you and across to the shoulder of the wave on the right-hand side. The streamlined shape of the canoe means that it will always gain enough speed to run ahead of any medium-sized wave and will have come to a standstill by the time the crest breaks over the canoeist. Hence the desirability of being able to swing to and fro on the wave to remain as long as possible on its slope. Another possibility, a favourite with board surfers, is to ride diagonally across the shoulder. This is entirely a question of balance. The paddle has no part to play at all, and the underwater shape of the canoe will decide the actual weight distribution which is called for.

ACROBATICS IN THE SURF

The board rider achieves manœuvrability by rapid shifts of weight. Moving his weight forward, he increases his speed down the slope of the wave. By standing on the starboard side, he increases underwater drag on that side and swings to starboard. Of course a very fine degree of balance and co-ordination is called for, which takes intensive practice to acquire. The canoeist, fixed in his seat, is clearly restricted, though he can make some small contribution by leaning forward or backward. (Canoe design varies too much to say that when a canoeist leans to starboard, his canoe will swerve in that direction. The opposite may be the case.) The canoeist's great advantage is the ability to perform a number of acrobatics which rely on the firm attachment of canoe and canoeist to one another.

The Forward Loop
The easiest to learn, and always exciting. Often happens involuntarily, but can also be done deliberately if the waves are big enough (about three feet). Ride a wave straight and keep the canoe on the steepest part of the wave by back paddling. Do not run ahead. As the wave is about to break the bow will go under. Hold the canoe straight, throw your weight forward. Over you go in a somersault; roll up again. Easiest in a canoe with slim bows and a light stern, the art is to go over vertically, to avoid swinging sideways at an angle.

Nose Diving
Identical with the forward loop, and easiest in a large but not a powerful surf. The canoe rises to the vertical position on its nose, then falls back again, seawards. Practice, and leaning slightly to one side as the canoe rises, will bring the canoe down parallel with the waves, and the paddle acting as a steadying outrigger, the canoe having thus achieved a 90-degree turn. Further practice on exactly the same lines will bring the canoe through 180 degrees and facing seawards as it comes down, the canoeist remaining clear of the water the whole time.

A variation of the Forward Loop, but best practised after the Nose Dive has been mastered, is to capsize as the bow buries itself. The canoe will loop and the canoeist finds himself sitting upright facing out to sea. The timing for this is very difficult.

The Backward Loop
Facing the waves, paddle backwards, keep the canoe head on to the surf by short forward strokes as the wave breaks; the stern will, with luck, bury itself and the canoe loop backwards. It is a sudden, sometimes unpleasant, sensation, particularly in heavy surf. It may happen anyway as you are trying to paddle out. No other manœuvre imposes a greater strain on the boat, and the after-deck of a strongly built fibre-glass canoe is frequently completely fractured and stove in by the jack-knife motion involved.

The variation of this loop, sometimes referred to as the

F

Eskimo Loop Proper, or Genuine Eskimo Loop, involves a capsize as the canoe begins to loop, with the canoeist finishing upright and able to continue surfing down the same wave. Really skilful timing can lead to the canoeist completing this feat without his head or body ever entering the water. Seen performed in an Eskimo kayak, on the front of a large green wave, it is a most graceful spectacle and has the touch of real artistry.

Further skills will surely be developed as the sport grows, and there must already be many surf canoeists with their own favourite variations.

RIDING GREEN WAVES

Continuously fighting against powerful white water is tiring, and on a day when the surf is really heavy, the good canoeist will prefer to spend his time beyond the breaking surf, riding the greenbacks. Sliding down the side of a wave which is inclined at 35 degrees, has a length three or four times that of a canoe, and is moving at 20 knots, is surely the supreme thrill for the canoe surfer. Racing down the face of these waves, it is possible to swing to left and right by shifts of balance and use of the paddle as a stern rudder. A start has been made in this country on formation surfing, and the sight of four or five canoeists performing in unison on these large waves is intensely thrilling. As they approach the moment when the wave breaks, they turn and climb off the crest to go out again for another run.

Two points remain to be mentioned in connection with heavy surf. First, in being carried sideways in the white water, the low telemark is a less fatiguing and often much more effective bracing stroke than the high telemark. It imposes a better weight distribution into the wave, whereas the high telemark, in addition to tending to lift the canoeist out of his cockpit, throws considerable strain on arm and thigh muscles. Secondly, in going out through powerful surf, the canoeist must keep his paddle in continuous use, never, for example, laying it alongside his foredeck or holding it high above his head. This is to preserve both forward motion and balance. If you are picked up and carried backwards, capsize, and roll up and carry on when the wave has let go of you. If you think you are going to be carried backwards, capsize before the wave hits you. This is an old and recognized method used by the Eskimos and also as a standard technique by board surfers.

THE ESKIMO ROLL

Arriving in Greenland in 1930 at the start of the British Arctic Air Route Expedition which he was leading, Gino Watkins, the young Polar explorer who tragically lost his life at the age of twenty-five, admired the grace and dexterity with which the Eskimos fell over in their kayaks, and, with a quick movement of the paddle, came up again on the other side. He soon realized his party would only be able to hunt seals by learning to kayak proficiently; further, that this manœuvre, far from being a mere circus trick, was an essential technique for survival.

Trying to swim in those icy waters, one died very quickly. So the Eskimos chose a narrow boat, which was unstable the right way up and unstable the wrong way up too, and therefore easily uprighted by the kayakist held firmly in his craft and using this paddle-stroke we call the Eskimo roll. Kayaks of this kind, blown off the coast by a sudden gale, have been waveridden from Greenland to Iceland and canoe and canoeist have survived, superb examples of human skill, fitness and suitability of boat for the environment.

Gino Watkins' party were not the first Europeans to master the Eskimo kayak; Fritjof Nansen and his companion Johansen had used them in their fantastic fifteen-month journey to Franz Josef Land in 1895–6, after their ship *The Fram* had been frozen into the North Polar Ocean. But now this skill, which, thanks to outboard engines, is rapidly disappearing from Greenland, has become an everyday feature of high-class sporting canoeing in this country, on the Continent, and increasingly too in Canada and the United States. A few years ago, a canoe-rolling demonstration was an exciting novelty at a riverside fête or a swimming gala. Nowadays, so many young people are learning to roll their canoes with their hands alone, that no public performance is complete unless this skill is included.

Although the Eskimo Roll is not perhaps of quite the same life-saving importance to the modern canoeist as it was to the East Greenlanders, one school of canoe coaches maintains that it ought to be one of the first skills taught to the novice canoeist who is old enough and strong enough to have any chance of success. Why?

1. A canoeist who can roll his canoe up again from the fully inverted position will, it follows, be able to recover from any intermediate position. He learns thereby the Eskimo's lesson that the expert canoeist depends for his stability in difficult water, not on any barge-like stability built into his canoe (quite the contrary), but on the use he makes of his paddle and the degree to which his canoe is part of him. Any spectator who spends five minutes at a canoe slalom competition will appreciate this point.

2. Learning to canoe well must involve many dozens of capsizes. The more advanced the stroke, or the more difficult the water, the more likely the capsize. The simple ability to roll saves time and energy otherwise spent swimming to the shore and emptying one's canoe.

3. Lack of inhibitions about capsizing brings aggressive confidence in learning the other techniques.

4. It is a safety factor of major importance. The advantages of having canoeists always able to rescue themselves are self-evident. The attitude towards water safety developed in young people who are learning to roll is invariably a sound one—familiarity here breeds respect.

5. The roll is an exciting and a precise challenge. Whilst many canoe skills can only be judged relatively, either one can roll or one can't; one comes up, or one doesn't. Furthermore, there are several types of roll which can be learnt one after the other in order of difficulty. A progressive ladder of achievement is provided.

6. Many canoeists have to wait for the week-end or for the holidays to travel to suitable canoeing water; but they may have a swimming pool near their home. The roll is an advanced technique which can be practised and improved for many enjoyable hours in a few square feet of water, and a real step is being taken towards greater proficiency under more rigorous white water conditions. Canoeing can carry on through the winter!

7. The Eskimo roll imposes a high standard of equipment. The newcomer to the sport who has been introduced to it via the Eskimo roll is unlikely to accept anything less than the best thereafter.

Of course, it is all too easy to become an indoor canoeist who is expert only in the clear, pleasant waters of the heated swimming pool; and who practises the roll purely as a stunt for the entertainment of wide-eyed spectators. It is vital that every opportunity be taken of transferring the swimming pool skill to cold water, fast-running rivers and breaking surf on the seashore. Then the whole technique is seen in its proper perspective and in its proper rôle.

Mastering the Technique

The prime aim in learning the Eskimo roll must be to master the technique which will bring you up with minimum effort in bad conditions and when you are tired—most people will manage to get up once or twice on brute force, but energy is quickly spent under water. You have to achieve two things:

1. Turn the boat the right way up.
2. Lift your body out of the water.

Both Archimedes Law and our experience tell us that a canoeist who may be eleven stone (154 lb.) out of water and quite a weight to lift with the paddle, in the water is virtually weightless. It is clear we must work with the water, not against it. The accompanying series of sketches shows how (Fig. 16).

Row A is what the roll looks like to the casual onlooker. The canoeist never alters his own position in relation to the canoe, and success is only achieved through rigid, tiring muscular effort.

Row B is the canoeist who lacks confidence under water and rushes his head up to the surface for air. Between *B.3* and *B.4* he is not only supporting the whole weight of his body on his paddle; he is dragging the canoe up after him as well. The expression on his face in *B.5* is one, not of achievement, but of intense relief after a difficult struggle.

Row C is the expert who has the confidence to keep his head under water until he has almost completed his roll. First he allows the water to carry his body up to the surface; then, in *C.3*, with a flexible twist of the hips, he flips his canoe past the critical point of stability as the lower gunwale begins to rise to the surface. From this moment onwards (*C.4*), the canoe itself is helping the canoeist up, and from here only a small push with the paddle is needed to lift the canoeist's body to the fully upright position. This is the vital principle which has to be grasped and practised; without it, the most difficult roll of all, with the hands alone, is impossible. The look on the face of our

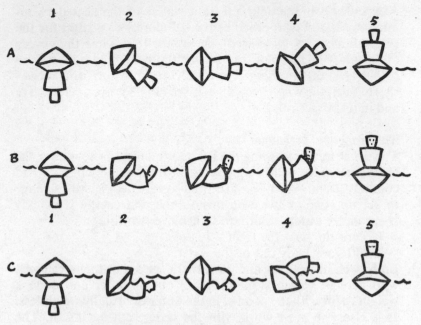

Fig. 16   The Eskimo Roll—working *with* the water, not *against* it

expert canoeist is one of complacent satisfaction—he has done it all so often before. The roll correctly performed involves so little muscular fatigue that a good canoeist, playing around in the swimming pool for an hour or so, will perform anything between 50 and 100 rolls without any appreciable fatigue whatever.

Flipping the boat over with one's hips is not too difficult if correctly done. Note that our expert roller is facing the water, with his shoulders parallel to the surface, as his boat rises. You will understand this at once if you sit on the floor, your legs out in front of you as though you were in a canoe. Try touching the floor with your right shoulder, at the same time keeping your seat firmly on the ground. Anatomically impossible, because your lower rib at once comes into collision with your pelvis! Now twist your trunk to the right and try again. You may not touch the floor with your forehead, but you will get much nearer to it than you did with your shoulder. The fact is that the Eskimo roll in still water is not a difficult thing to achieve. Most people who fail to roll after four or five training sessions are entitled to sack their instructor. Which brings us to the various types of roll and the methods of learning them.

Learn the Pawlata First

Experts still differ about which roll to teach the novice first, but most of the relevant arguments suggest the Pawlata, mainly because it can be learned as a drill movement, and because it is a useful and practical roll for all water conditions. Whichever roll is taken first, certain points must be observed.

1. Never practise or allow anyone to learn or practise on his own. Not only is this dangerous, but he or she will inevitably learn bad habits. A good rolling technique can be acquired in as little as ten minutes; bad habits will often take literally months to cure.

2. Learning the roll demands absolute concentration from both the learner and the instructor. Ten minutes is as long as most learners can really concentrate, slightly longer if conditions are favourable (indoor pool, heated water), shorter if outside in the cold.

3. The roll is best taught in shallow water, between 2 ft 6 in. and 3 ft 6 in. deep. The instructor must be able to move quickly and to right his pupil immediately and without difficulty. Teaching the roll from another canoe is highly inefficient in time spent and results gained.

4. Equipment needed: A satisfactory canoe, that is, a slalom or white water boat, fitted with a watertight spray cover, a firm seat which fits the canoeist tightly, knee-rests, preferably adjustable, and a strong foot rest which must be adjustable. The modern white water canoeist does not sit in his canoe; he wears it like a pair of tight-fitting trousers. Get two people to hold a steel bar for the canoeist to pull himself up on. Does the canoe slip? Can he wriggle it about with his hips? Incidentally, many wood and canvas canoes will need strengthening around the cockpit if they are to take the strain of rolling. Glass-fibre canoes are best but also expensive.

The narrow-beamed Eskimo kayak is still frequently used for teaching rolling. It is too easy. Correct technique is not important enough for successful rolling in it. Moving into a slalom or white water boat, the learner is likely to have to start all over again. Much sounder practice is to begin straight away in the slightly more difficult type of boat.

To complete the equipment, a paddle with blades feathered at right angles to one another, and with a strong shaft, preferably of aluminium. Some find a face mask helpful, and nose clips certainly prevent water entering the nose.

There is more than one method of teaching the Pawlata Roll. The following notes outline a method which has been used successfully, without variation, in at least 150 cases.

1. Put the learner in his canoe without a paddle and tell him to capsize and swim to the side, still 'wearing' his canoe. Insist on the breast stroke to get the trunk into the right position for the hip movement described above. If he comes out of his canoe, start again and persist until he does it calmly and confidently.

2. Give the learner the paddle to hold at one end and hold the other end, blade horizontal, at water level yourself. Make him lean over until elbow, then shoulder, then ear touches the water, and then level himself up on the paddle. Do this (to ear standard) six times to port and six to starboard. Make him keep the canoe at right angles to the paddle all the time.

3. Give him the paddle to himself and make him do the same as in (2), using the flat blade on the water instead of on your hand. Don't go on to the next stage until he has done this six times successfully to port and six times successfully to starboard. Don't let him capsize altogether while practising this as nothing is learnt and time is wasted.

4. Take away his paddle, make him fold his arms and lean slightly forward. Stand just behind him on the port side, roll him to upside down, count three and roll him up again. If he falls out, or does not seem to enjoy it, go on doing it until he hardly notices. Once is often enough.

5. Make him put his paddle in the Pawlata teaching position, paddle fore and aft along the deck on the port side, forward blade flat on the foreward deck, right hand near the middle of the loom, back of hand uppermost, left hand gripping the end of the after blade round the end, back of hand outboard. Tell him to lean forward and keep the blade there. Roll him to upside down, count three, and roll him up again. If the paddle has moved, go on doing it until he has learnt to keep it where he was told.

6. Teach him while upright to put the paddle over the side to the surface of the water, maintaining it fore and aft close to the boat, and forward blade still at the 30-or-so-degree angle of the foredeck. Tell him to put it back on deck. Then 'over the side', 'on deck', 'over the side', 'on deck', etc., until he never makes a mistake with his eyes shut.

7. Teach him, from the 'over the side' position, the stroke sweeping the forward end of the paddle in an arc out to the left

and then transversely up over his right shoulder. Take the paddle away and explain what actually happens when the stroke is done, while the canoe starts to roll up, how the resultant movements of body and paddle lead to the blade of the latter being swept around on the surface of the water, and why it is necessary as the head emerges from the water to alter one's muscle movements so as to force the body upright. Illustrate the fact that if the paddle is pulled round the chest, a common fault, instead of being swept up over the shoulder, then, as the head of the canoeist surfaces, the paddle will be vertically down instead of still on the surface.

8. Practise the paddle movements—'on deck', pause, 'over the side', pause, stroke, 'on deck', pause, 'over the side', pause, and stroke, over and over again, with the eyes shut, until never a mistake is made. Teach the canoeist to feel with the eyes shut the correct position of the paddle on the surface of the water at 'over the side' by the impact of the fingers of the left hand and thumb of the right hand on the gunwale edge of the canoe.

9. Stand just to rear of canoeist on the port side and let him have a go for himself. If he makes any mistake with paddle drill, go back to drilling on the surface again. If he makes no mistakes, he is certain to contribute largely to the roll, and the instructor has only to flick the boat up with his fingers. The pupil must normally be told at this stage that he has not used enough force in his stroke. He should not be permitted to attempt more than about six rolls on his first lesson unless he is doing it right all the time. Otherwise he will get worse and get discouraged.

Faults

1. Much the most common faults are those of the instructor who does not insist on perfect performance at each separate stage of training before moving on to the next. The most common fault of all is inadequate attention to the fit of the canoeist in his canoe. Such faults on the part of the instructor can delay excessively the achievement of the roll and discourage unduly the canoeist. Nine out of ten canoeists should *almost* roll by themselves at the *first* attempt, needing only a little flick of assistance by the instructor. More than one in three should roll entirely by themselves on the first attempt even though they will fail many times when practising later.

2. Instructors must stand in the right place, which, when teaching the roll to the left (normal for right-handed people), is

port side immediately behind the canoeist. This is the safe place for the instructor and the one where he can best roll the boat or help it round without straining. The instructor should not normally touch the canoeist at all. Many don't like being clutched round the chest, and in the case of females the action may be misconstrued.

3. Young and slight boys should have even more attention paid to their drill, over and over again with each stage of the training, until they are perfect, *before* they are allowed to try their first roll. It is especially important for them to avoid a succession of 'failed rolls'. Since they are light and easily managed, it is a good thing to simulate the last half of the roll with the instructor holding the canoe at the half-roll position 90 degrees to upright and then letting the boy finish the roll. This is the half of the stroke in which failure is most common.

4. The more middle-aged canoeist sometimes is *nearly* successful with his first few attempts and then seems to get stuck at that stage. It is often due to drill fixation and failure to appreciate that in the second half of the roll one must consciously change from pulling oneself up, as at the start, to pushing oneself up as at the finish. This sort of mind-muscular complex is occasionally very difficult indeed to break, but perseverance will win through in the end. There is no moderately fit, confident in water, human being, who cannot roll a canoe under the easy conditions of the swimming bath, tall or short, fat or thin, young or old.

Subsequent Training

As soon as the canoeist can Pawlata roll successfully in the bath on every occasion, he should be made to throw his paddle away, then swim to it in his canoe, put it in place and roll up. Failures here are usually the result of wrong placement, especially angle, of paddle blade. It is common to put the forward blade *too* vertical, over-correction of an earlier fault, having it too flat and then finding it will not swing round. Canoeists must be taught to take a breath immediately their head breaks water. It is very easy to forget, and after a couple of failed rolls, one has then to leave the canoe for air quite unnecessarily.

The common desire to move on to other types of roll before 100 per cent reliability with the Pawlata has been achieved should be resisted. Complete reliability includes going out and performing it in rough and cold water, on rivers, lakes or in the sea. There will be disappointment at first, but practice will soon bring the confidence necessary for success under the new conditions.

NOTE. All the above instructions, and the remarks on the rolls which follow, apply to the right-hander, who normally capsizes to the left and rolls up on the right. For the left-hander, everything should be reversed.

It is worth emphasizing here how important it is for the would-be expert to learn to perform every roll with complete ease on both sides. The aim must be to recover instinctively and at once on whichever side one is falling over.

The Put Across Roll
Still sometimes taught as a beginner's roll, but of little use in running water as the paddle is quickly swept out of position; it is, however, useful in teaching orientation under water and the all-important flexible movement of the hips.

Method: Hold the paddle at right angles across the cockpit, the left blade vertical. Capsize to the left. Hanging underneath, pass the paddle across under the canoe and allow it to float to the surface on the opposite side to the side of the capsize. The far blade must lie flat on the surface. With the left hand grasping the edge of the vertical blade and the right hand about a third the paddle's length from the left hand, lever upwards by pulling down briskly with the right hand. As the stroke is being completed, draw the paddle into the chest.

A helpful alternative for those who have difficulty is to lay the paddle out on the surface on the right hand side, then to fall towards the paddle, grasping it as described above, and levering upwards at once. Fall over each time a little further.

Common faults: Paddle not at right-angles to the canoe. Outer blade not parallel to the surface. Head raised before hips.

The Steyr
Not an Eskimo, but a European roll, developed in Steyr, Austria. Very attractive to watch, mainly an exhibition roll. Basically the Pawlata done over the stern of the canoe instead of the bow.

Method: Place the paddle at right angles across the cockpit, the right-hand blade lying flat on the water, right hand one-third of the paddle's length down the loom, left hand grasping the end of the left-hand blade. Capsize to the left. In capsizing, twist the trunk to face the stern, bring the paddle in a swift, cartwheel motion to enter the water at the stern of the canoe at the very moment of capsize. Before the paddle enters the water, drop the right wrist and lead into the water with the right forearm and what was the underside of the right blade in the starting position. Continue the circular paddle motion, pushing upwards off the surface. Draw paddle into the chest and finish lying along the stern deck.

Common faults: Incorrect angle of entry of the paddle into the water. Entry of blade too far from the stern of the canoe. Paddle drops below the surface during the recovery. A break in what should be one continuous movement from start to finish. Many canoeists tend to complete their Steyr roll with an off-beat variation of the Put Across.

The Screw
Incomparably the most useful, also one of the most difficult rolls; most useful because there is no repositioning of the hands, and the canoeist can recover at once from the completely inverted or any intermediate position; the most difficult because the hands remaining in the basic paddling position, the lever provided by the paddle is much shorter. This is the roll which reveals good or bad basic technique. A 'must' for the slalom canoeist for whom speed is essential.

Method: Exactly as for the Pawlata, except that the hands remain in the normal paddling position. Whilst in learning it is permissible to capsize with the paddle in the prepared Pawlata position, the purpose of the roll is immediate recovery from any position, and this should be practised intensively.

Common faults: Incorrect angle of the outer blade. This is eventually corrected by instinct, but if in trouble, slide the left hand back along the shaft to the left hand blade to enable you to correct the angle. This also increases the length of paddle leverage and wastes little time. Left-hand blade caught up against the gunwale—It is vital to swing out from the boat and along the surface with the right hand and blade.

The Reverse Screw
The Steyr Roll performed with the hands in the normal, or Screw, position. A neat roll, economical in effort, and an excel-

lent test of the canoeist's flexibility. Mainly an exhibition roll, but the recovery part of it is used in preference to other recoveries by a fair number of canoeists. A good preparation roll for learning to roll with the hands.

Vertical Paddle Roll

In effect this roll is nothing more than the Put Across Roll with the paddle placed vertically instead of horizontally. To the onlooker it looks as if the canoeist is pushing off the bottom; to the canoeist who has mastered the other rolls it is quite astonishingly easy.

Method: The canoeist hangs upside down under his canoe, places the paddle in a vertical position, the top blade just sticking out of the water beside his cockpit, and at right angles to his gunwale, the left hand curled over the top edge of the uppermost blade, the right hand grasping the paddle shaft in a comfortable position about halfway down. A brisk jerk inwards with the right hand will bring the canoeist up. With practice the direction of the jerk can easily be varied.

A much more useful variation is obtained by again keeping the hands in the normal paddling position. This roll provides a useful illustration of rolling expertise encouraging basic stroke proficiency. On the draw stroke learners are always reluctant to dig their blades in deeply. This in fact makes for greater, not less, stability, as well as for more power in moving sideways.

The Strap Hang

Also known by other names. An exhibition trick, but also useful practice. The canoeist leaves his paddle floating alongside his right gunwale, capsizes to the left and, putting his right hand on either of the paddle blades or on the paddle loom, pulls up with a brisk movement. Useful practice is obtained by varying the position of the paddle before capsizing. The further the paddle is pushed towards the stern, the more valuable the practice.

The Hat Trick

A pure demonstration stunt, easily achieved with practice, but effective entertainment. As the canoeist capsizes (to the left), he places an appropriate piece of headgear (for schoolboy performers, mortar-boards; for naval cadets, a high-ranking peaked cap; for you and me, an impressive topper) on the upturned bottom of his canoe with his left hand. Swimming carefully round to the other side, he reaches for the hat, again with his left hand, and, keeping both hand and hat out of the water, returns to the upright position. Suitable recoveries are the Pawlata, the Put Across and the Vertical Paddle.

Rolling by Hand

Gino Watkins learned this trick from the Eskimos, and it is becoming more and more common in this country today. Whilst it may not be of direct use, except in the extreme circumstances of a canoeist capsizing and losing his paddle, when he can normally be rescued by fellow canoeists anyway, it has immense value in providing an ultimate target for the roller, in perfecting his body movements, and in developing really high-class confidence underwater. It should definitely be regarded as more than an exhibition stunt.

The canoeist who has mastered all the above techniques has gone most of the way towards this one; but additional preparation is achieved by rolling with, say, a table-tennis bat, or, better still, with a piece of wood which is shortened inch by inch as proficiency increases. Use the Steyr technique for preference. In the early stages, lean right back against the afterdeck when capsizing—here the more modern slalom boat in which the lower part of the seat is set forward from the backrest, or the Eskimo kayak with its flat afterdeck, are helpful. You need a flexible spine! With your head underwater, twist the boat as far over as possible with the hips, pushing hard with the right knee; then, sweep from stern to bow along the surface with the right hand, swinging the left hand over the left gunwale to provide a counter-weight. The most common fault is to allow the head to swing out at right angles, and its extended weight then pulls the boat down again. Keep the head as far back as possible against the afterdeck, though turning it sideways to allow free hip movement. Co-ordination and rhythm are vital, and it is helpful in the early stages to make use of the initial downward momentum. This later becomes unnecessary.

There are other ways of performing this roll. Some canoeists prefer to strike down with the left hand first to assist with the initial hip movement. Others prefer the Pawlata to the Steyr approach. Common to all is the hip movement, and indeed, so flexible does the practised hand roller become, that even the head position can become comparatively unimportant. Some canoeists have achieved the roll using only the right hand, with the left hand tucked in the spray cover. The last target to be achieved is the roll with no hands, using only body movement. To my knowledge, no one has ever achieved this yet, but I have seen a slalom canoe moved up to its point of balance, standing on its gunwale, by body movement alone, so perhaps even this extraordinary feat may soon be accomplished, though some suspension of the Laws of Mechanics would seem to be necessary.

Every experienced canoeist will point out that the ability to roll, even to roll in difficult water, does not by itself produce an expert canoeist. But, inevitably, the competent roller will have gained so much confidence, so much general expertise, that he will be (provided he is sensible in other respects, like not canoeing alone) an eminently safe canoeist. Not least, his skill with the paddle will have so improved his reflexes and his recovery strokes that he will rarely capsize. He will have adopted his own preferred roll, perhaps a combination of two standard ones (a favourite here is a combination of the Put Across and the Reverse Screw) and he will have learnt to roll by preference against the direction of moving water—on the sea by rolling into the waves; if broadside on a river, by rolling upstream against the current; if facing downstream, by using a Steyr or Reverse Screw; if facing upstream, a Pawlata or ordinary screw. But the more proficient the canoeist, the shorter his rolling stroke becomes and the more it appears to be nothing more than a swift lunge with the paddle, and the faster the water is running, the less the effort required.

Finally, one curious fact may be mentioned. Those who learn the roll quickly, forget it quickly. Some may take wearisome hours to learn it, but the unfailing hallmark of their rolling in the end is its utter reliability.

6

Slalom and White Water Racing

JULIAN SHAW

WELL. Here we go. Deep breath now. Swoosh. The canoe hurtles down the sluice and drives beneath the stopper which is gnashing its teeth in expectation. The world slows down, the green turns to white, and all of a sudden the lungs are thankful for the skill of their owner.

How can we describe the exhilaration of pitting one's skill against the tricks of a rapid river. It is the challenge offered by such a river which demands the epitome of canoeing ability and watermanship and leads us to wild water racing and slalom.

Slalom was first introduced to Britain by Frank Sutton, who came to this country from Austria. With the assistance of the Manchester Canoe Club he organized an event at Trevor Rocks on the River Dee in 1939. This was supported by three or four people from London, several from the Midlands, one from Newcastle, and nearly the whole strength of the Manchester club. Rather than using poles suspended from overhead wires as the artificial obstacles, pieces of cork tied on the end of string were tried. These had the regrettable tendency of twizzling round a paddle shaft as soon as they were touched, which resulted in only five competitors finishing the course.

The second event was held in Ludlow in the following year, but there was then a gap until 1948, when the BCU gave its blessing to an event at Tymean Island, again on the Dee. Since then growth has been phenomenal, with some of our major events now attracting over 150 competitors.

Canoe slalom is primarily a challenge against the water and the elements, and as such is held in fairly hazardous conditions. It is quite usual for the experts to travel as far afield as the north of Scotland or similar remote parts to find a course of sufficient difficulty. However, it is realized that it would be foolhardy to allow beginners on to such water and therefore all the major slaloms, and competitors, are divided into a number of divisions. Naturally, as the numbers taking part have increased, so

6. Cruising on the River Hornad in Czechoslovakia

7. The massed start of a long distance race

8. Portaging past a lock during a long distance race

the number of divisions has increased. In 1965 we had four full divisions plus a Novices division.

At the start of each season clubs who want their slaloms to be recognized events apply to the BCU Slalom Committee for ranking status. Once this has been granted, the club concerned has to run the slalom to the standards laid down, but in return will get help regarding score-sheets, timing apparatus, loud-hailers, etc.

Everybody starts in the Novices division, but after competing in two such events is automatically moved up into division four. From here, however, promotion and relegation depends on one's performance. A win at any event results in immediate promotion to the division above, but otherwise both promotion and relegation occur at the end of the season when positions in the annual ranking list have been worked out. Precise details of the ranking list can be found from the combined *Diary and Year Book* which is published each year by the Slalom Committee.

Not only does the divisional system enable organizers to give our international standard men in division one a course which will test them to the full, but it also means that everyone will be able to find a competitition of just the right standard. No doubt this is one of the reasons why we have risen from being little more than observers in 1949 to winning the World Championship in 1959. Paul Farrant's win at Geneva in 1959 showed that we had been working on the right lines, and our third place in the team event in 1963 proved that we can get not one but three men to the very top.

On the international scene the supremacy has moved slowly from the Austrians and Swiss, to Czechoslovakia, to West Germany and now to East Germany. One gets the impression that although the overall standard has been going up all the time, we in Britain have been gaining on the rest of Europe. So far America and Canada have been out of the running, but over there too slalom is now catching on.

EQUIPMENT

Of critical importance to the white water canoeist is his equipment. While it is true that the results will depend more on the man than on his equipment, it has to be remembered that, in a very heavy rapid, life and limb may be at stake.

The design of a slalom canoe is most complex; one might

G

almost call it a compromise of compromises. The designer of a K1 racing kayak has one objective: speed. All else can be subordinated to that end. When we look at a slalom canoe there are five basic design features which have to be considered.

1. MANŒUVRABILITY. This most essential quality can be secured either by having a short waterline or by having a rockered keel (i.e. rising towards bow and stern). Both solutions have the desired effect but only at the expense of speed and acceleration. Very flat sections, which also favour manœuvrability, have the same unfortunate effects and in addition they impair effective stability.

2. SPEED is secured by a long waterline, narrow V section and pronounced straight keel. Quite the opposite to the features demanded for manœuvrability.

3. ACCELERATION. When you consider how often in a slalom or on a rapid river you have to reverse direction, the importance of this quality will become apparent. By far the most important requirement for this is lightness. Two things must be borne in mind; a very manœuvrable boat will never have good acceleration due to yawing, and a very light boat feels alarmingly lively at first and needs getting used to.

4. INHERENT STABILITY. To most people a stable boat is a broad flat one. While it is true that such a boat will sit upright on flat water, it is a completely different situation in rough water. A boat with a flat section will conform to the water surface. Thus on a sloping surface, such as on a wave, a boat with a kipper-box cross section will tip over and be uncontrollable. Inherent stability is a very much overrated quality.

5. EFFECTIVE STABILITY. The Eskimo kayak has this to a remarkable degree due to its narrowness and low centre of gravity. In other words a boat which can be rolled easily.

There is one further feature which is of even greater significance and this is the seating position, It is no use having a superb boat and knowing the river like the back of your hand if the seating position leaves something to be desired. It is insufficient merely to sit on or in a slalom canoe. One has to become part of it and behave as a unified combination. The novice may detect that the water is having a certain effect on the canoe and apply a corrective stroke. This will come far too late. With a correct seating position such movements can be anticipated and allowed for even before they have begun. Not only is the sensing done by the seating position but so is the control. This is exercised through (a) your feet resting on a rigid foot-rest, (b) your knees or thighs under the coaming and (c) your sit-upon parked on a rigid seat. Any movement of the boat must be immediately transferred to the body, and vice versa.

Thus the paddler should be wedged in tightly but comfortably. A position which leads to pins-and-needles should be corrected.

Completing the boat is the spray-cover. This should allow plenty of free movement for the trunk, should not come off accidentally, but with ease in an emergency; and of course it should also be waterproof. These are the usual requirements, but each one must be taken to the extreme for the more critical conditions.

The next item of interest is the paddle. Of universal acceptance is that it should be between 6 ft 8 in. and 7 ft long; it should be feathered at 90 degrees; it should be light yet strong. To go further than this is to step into a field of controversy. For many years flat blades have been used. The reason for this is that so much back-paddling is used that a curved blade loses its advantage. Recently the spoon blade has come back into favour. It does have tremendous advantages when paddling forwards but demands plenty of practice if bracing techniques are to be used in turbulent water.

Another area of discussion is that of blade size. A large blade is efficient but both clumsy and high-geared. A smaller one 'slips' a little and gives the effect of lower gearing and consequently better acceleration.

The two other items considered to be necessities are life-jacket and crash helmet. Plenty has been written about the safety aspect. The expert canoeist becomes very familiar with the various water conditions but at no time should this familiarity breed contempt. It is a sign of the expert that he should be able to recognize a potential danger.

STROKES

In canoeing there are two different classes of strokes. First of all there is the straightforward paddling action which is described in detail in another chapter; then there are the sweep strokes also covered in the section detailing the basic techniques. But to the slalomist there is a more important group, possibly better referred to as Braces. The whole art of rough water canoeing is to let the water do the work for you. We therefore have a whole selection of paddle positions which can be used to give different results from a given water condition. Not only is this desirable just from the viewpoint of saving effort, but it also ensures that no attempt will be made to emulate King Canute.

The most obvious manœuvre is to turn by paddling harder on one side. Very simple, of course, but in a slalom canoe we have a trick to enhance the performance. The gunwale has a much tighter curvature than the keel, and therefore, if the boat is tipped over through 90 degrees, the result will be to reduce the effective waterline. As we know, a shorter boat will turn more easily. Hence when turning, say, to the left by paddling hard on the right, we will tilt the boat over to the right.

The Telemark
This technique of reducing the effective waterline is also used in the telemark turn. The telemark involves nothing more than putting one blade into the water as a brake and spinning round it. As before, it will help to lean the boat but this time we shall lean to the inside of the turn. For the telemark to be as efficient as possible, the blade in the water must be vertical, so as to get a good purchase, but some force has to be applied to prevent our leaning resulting in a capsize. Accordingly, the blade is angled slightly so that the water pushing against it keeps it up on the surface and gives some stability (Fig. 17).

The High Telemark
With the telemark it is the back of the blade which is used to thrust against the water and this contrasts with the high telemark which involves turning the paddle over so that the normal working surface (the concave side of a spoon blade) faces forwards. Fig. 18 shows how the paddle is held above and slightly behind the head. The action of putting it behind the head automatically induces the blade reversal. Try it. The apparent complexity of the position belies its main virtue which, surprisingly enough, is stability.

The condition which causes a capsize is a sudden unexpected change in the wave formation. This is very frequent in the boil beneath a weir where little swirls can form and disperse with no warning whatsoever. If such an emergency should occur

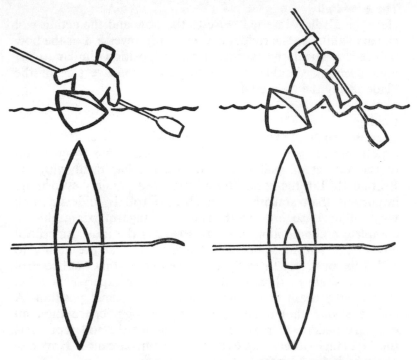

Fig. 17   The Telemark   Fig. 18   The High Telemark

during a telemark it will be difficult to counter, as the paddles
are restricted in movement—i.e. it cannot move aft due to one's
body being in the way, it cannot move downwards because of
the boat, and it cannot be lifted if the blade is immersed. At
least you have time to take a deep breath. In the case of the
high telemark the required freedom of action is retained and
one is never caught out in this way.

The Stern Rudder
In both forms of the telemark the paddle extends at right angles
to the boat level with the paddler. A more elementary technique
is to trail the paddle blade in the water close to the stern
letting it act as a rudder. As a rough-water boat has no pro-
truding keel, the action resulting from this is a gentle turn in
which the stern swings out in the required direction. On some
occasions this swing out could be an embarrassment and in
such cases we could resort to the bow pull.

The Bow Pull

Here the blade is inserted close to the bow and the action will be very similar to the rudder action, but in reverse. For the bow pull it is particularly important that a position similar to the high telemark should be used, with the concave side of the blade facing the stem post.

Rolling

Exercises such as the 'Colorado Hook' are better left to the expert, but the mere mention of such a technique brings us on to the subject of rolling. David Sutcliffe has dealt with the Eskimo Roll in the preceding chapter, but possibly even more important than actually being able to roll is understanding why rolling is so important. The advantage of being able to complete a competition after a capsize is the most superficial advantage. The most important feature is that the ability to roll is the only way to really convince oneself that boat control has to operate in three dimensions. To the expert a position over on the beam end is no longer an abnormal position. A rolling stroke should be of no greater significance than an ordinary paddling stroke. To the beginner the roll represents the first stage of learning even how to turn a canoe. How else could he judge how far to lean?

In some ways it is unfortunate that the telemark, high telemark, stern rudder and bow pull are all bracing rather than dynamic strokes. To practise them, most people will choose a swimming bath or stretch of smooth water, on which, having got up to high speed, they will lock themselves in their chosen position to complete the manœuvre.

Compare this with the slalomist's natural habitat. Imagine him coming down a sluice with the intention of breaking out behind a large boulder lying next to the fast stream. In readiness to turn, he will shoot the fall at a slight angle and it is easy to see that his bow will reach the eddy behind the eddy first. To help the bow to latch on to this stationary water the paddle will be put into the water in the bow pull position. However, as the boat gets further into the slack, the blade has to be moved further back into the high telemark position. The point to note is that as the boat is turning relative to the water forces, then the stroke required also changes. This is not the case in the artificial environment of the swimming pool.

So far we have made no mention of the 'Draw', 'Sideways

Sculling' or the 'Figure of Eight' Before attempting rough-water canoeing such techniques will have been mastered, as would any other basic operation. In boisterous conditions the inherent weakness of these strokes will make them of limited usefulness and many a slalom has been lost because they were used. Sideways movement should always be achieved by turning the boat and paddling in the required direction. A slalom boat is so easy to turn that a ferry glide action is frequently used.

As to the Eskimo Roll, there is a variety of methods, all of which should be practised as an exercise, but for all practical applications, the screw roll is the only one which need be considered.

For many years it was also considered necessary to roll on the 'downstream' side of the canoe in the belief that the current would also help. This may be the case when playing to an audience at a weir slalom, but on a river the inverted body quickly brings the capsized canoe to the same speed as the water, thus either side can be used for rolling.

The force which can be exerted by running water is tremendous, and it is this force which the expert has to learn first to respect and then to use for his own ends. Before examining the competitive aspect we must therefore learn some of the mysteries of the river, how to recognize them, and how to conquer them.

THE CHALLENGE OF FAST WATER

In this chapter we are only interested in moving water, but it is this movement which enables us to judge what is going on. Any object in the water will cause some disturbance, and the disturbance caused will depend on the speed of the water and the depth of the object. A quick look at Fig. 19 will show how a V-shaped wave formation is created in the lee of a rock. The rock itself may or may not be submerged, but on the surface the white area of disturbed water will reveal its position. Should there be a number of rocks there will be a number of white Vs; but to the canoeist the area between these Vs will in contrast appear as a black V guiding the way downstream. The larger the V the deeper and safer the channel.

Just behind each rock we find that the water is not being

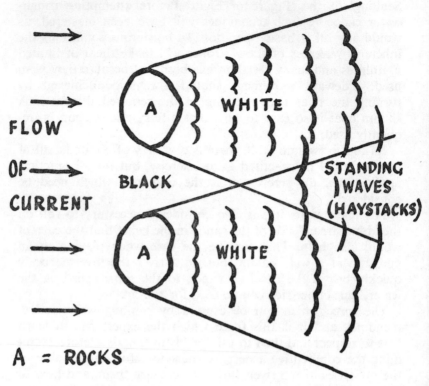

FLOW
OF
CURRENT

WHITE

A

BLACK

A

WHITE

STANDING
WAVES
(HAYSTACKS)

A = ROCKS

Fig. 19   How a V-shaped wave formation is created in the lee of a rock

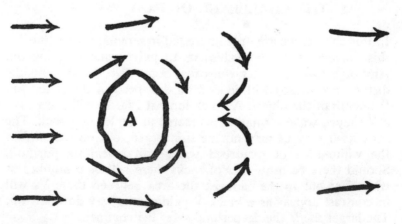

A

Fig. 20   The eddy current behind a rock

whisked off downstream but is possibly turning back on itself
and creating an eddy current (Fig. 20). Where our obstruction
is sufficiently pronounced to create a fall, this effect occurs
not only in the plan view but also as seen from the side. As the
river forces its way over a rock or pours over a weir it will
gather speed. However, as this fast water meets the static water
below, it will lose its energy and in so doing produce the wave
formations which are a delight to the canoeist. Only experience
can tell the rough-water canoeist how to recognize the difference
between a mound of water created by a submerged rock and the
wave created by fast water meeting slower moving water.

At the foot of a weir the fast water plunges to the bottom of
the river and then rebounds up again and curls back on itself.
The top of this curling wave actually flows upstream, and as the
water falls back once more it traps air bubbles to give the
characteristic white appearance (Fig. 21).

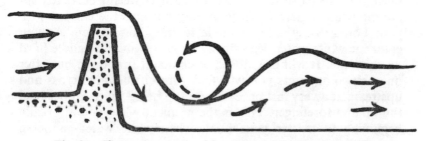

Fig. 21 The curling back of fast water at the foot of a weir

No matter what the conditions, whether runnels on a stream
or heavy falls on a mature river, the water will behave as
described. It cannot be stressed too often that the rough water
canoeist makes use of the water to help him.

The Ferry Glide
The most difficult thing for the novice to learn is how to move
successfully from slow to fast-moving water and back again.
It is all a question of balance and quick reactions. Let us take
the simplest possible case—the canoeist who wants to move
from one quiet bank through a strong current to the far quiet
bank. He can do this cautiously with the Ferry Glide. You
want to be more ambitious. Turn your boat at right angles to
the bank and paddle firmly into the current with your bow
turned only slightly upstream. Your instinct is to lean up-

stream. You will capsize at once, because the fast-moving current has swept your canoe from underneath you. Try again. This time, lean firmly downstream, using your paddle as a support. You will cross the strong current safely and must then only remember to lean upstream again as you enter the slower water. Practise crossing the stream in both directions until the unnatural reaction of leaning downstream has become a natural one.

The High Cross
The next stage is to combine this new principle of weight distribution with the Ferry Glide, thus moving on to the High Cross. Using the Ferry Glide, you cross a strong current by moving at right angles to the bank. With the High Cross you will cross the current and make ground upstream at the same time. Work your way up the quiet water at the side of the river until you are close to a rapid or to a powerful current containing white water. Work your way out into the current with your bow at only a slight angle to the main stream. As you enter the white water, lean firmly downstream and paddle hard on that side. It will probably not come off first time, but after one or two attempts you will find yourself moving across and upstream at a very fast pace—like a pip being squeezed between thumb and forefinger. This is the moment when you are really beginning to master your boat, when white water canoeing comes alive.

WILD WATER RACING AND SLALOM

The rough-water canoeist is of necessity a perfectionist and it is only natural that competitions should flourish. The most straightforward of these is the wild water race. The rules for this are very simple. The competitors leave the start at regular intervals, usually every two minutes, and are timed to the finish; the fastest man wins. No portages are allowed, and any man who is caught up by the boat behind has to give way to the faster boat. The only other rules concern safety and boat dimensions.

In complete contrast to this is slalom. Here the rules, so simple in outline, have become incredibly complicated in detail. Worse still, many interpretations of the rules are based on case history.

Wild water racing is purely a test of speed over a rough course. In slalom the course becomes a tortuous path embracing the most difficult, most rewarding water features. The competitor is now judged strictly on his ability to control his boat. Unlike figure skating, for instance, where specific movements have to be demonstrated, the slalom judge considers only what is achieved, not *how* it is achieved. On the other hand, the course designer will lay out a course which will enable a skilful competitor to save a lot of time by using a sophisticated technique.

As with the ordinary race, the competitors leave the start one at a time. On this occasion, however, their course is partially dictated by the presence of approximately twenty 'gates', through which they have to pass in the order in which they are numbered. All gates consist of two poles suspended from a wire stretched across the river. In most cases one of the poles will have green-and-white bands and the other one red-and-white bands. It is one of the basic rules that whenever the boat is between these poles the starboard side should face the green pole and the port side the red pole. Most gates will be tackled forwards unless a letter R has been hung next to the gate number, in which case it is necessary to pass through travelling stern first. The other type of gate is one which uses a pair of black-and-white poles. The only requirement here is that the competitor should pass between the poles. He can choose whether he does so forwards or backwards or even upside down!

Penalties
The object of the exercise is to pass through the gate without touching it. Failure to do so results in a penalty, expressed in seconds, which is added to the time taken.

A 10 seconds' penalty is added if one of the poles is touched by the boat, body or paddle while passing through the gate. Repeated touching of the same pole does not increase the penalty.

A 20 seconds' penalty is awarded if both the poles are touched as above.

A 50 seconds' penalty is awarded if the competitor or his boat collides with the gate (either or both poles) on his way through.

A competitor is considered to be attempting a gate as soon as he, or any part of his boat, has crossed the imaginary line between the poles or has touched the pole(s). To avoid the last penalty of 50 seconds both bow, foredeck and body must cross this line.

A 50 seconds' penalty is also awarded for wrong presentation (i.e. doing a forward gate backwards or presenting the wrong gunwale to one of the coloured poles).

A 100 seconds' penalty is incurred if a gate is omitted entirely.

These conditions are all quite straightforward and would present no difficulties during a well-controlled run. But in practice there are many problems, for when a slalomist gets himself into trouble he has more to do than wonder whether he is making things easy for the judges. The boat may pass under one of the poles. If it does so without touching (due to the pole being hung higher than it ought to be) the competitor gets away without penalty. If there is a touch, the canoeist is liable to one of the penalties above.

Another difficulty is that of deciding when a competitor has omitted a gate. It is decreed that when a competitor appears to have missed a gate, the 100 seconds' penalty will be imposed as soon as he attempts the following gate.

As an example of this, consider a man who has done gate 1 and has insufficient skill to reach gate 2. After failing to get to gate 2 he will pass on to gate 3. As soon as he attempts gate 3 (touches or crosses line) the judge will impose the 100 seconds' penalty for gate 2. This is the simple case.

In contrast, assume that our competitor, after doing gate 1, accidentally hits gate 3 while paddling towards gate 2. To the judge, who is not a mind reader, this is an identical situation, and he instantly imposes the identical penalty. Thus for a competitor it is necessary to consider the gate about to be attempted and also the one immediately following it.

Course Conditions

We are now in a position to have a look at a typical course and, as would be the case for an organizer or a competitor, we will look first at the water conditions. With the aid of Fig. 22 imagine a weir over which the water flows at one point only. This will produce a narrow jet of fast water with an area of slack at either side. As we move further from the weir the fast water will slow down and spread out. The effect of the bulge

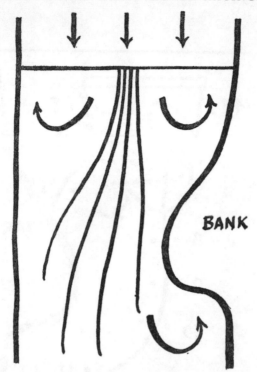

Fig. 22   An example of the flow of water over a weir, and the effect on
it of a bulge in the river bank

on the left bank will be to swing the mainstream over to the
opposite bank. There will be an eddy in the lee of the bulge
which will be stronger than the eddies close to the weir.

An example of a suitable course (very short) on this water is
Fig. 23. From the start the competitor will paddle up through
gate 1 and will then have to turn for gate 2R. It is imperative
that this turn be made in an anti-clockwise direction. Doing it
this way the current will do all the work. In attempting to turn
the other way, not only will assistance be lacking, but the
current will be acting in opposition. The same considerations
will apply when turning for gate 3. The passage from here across
to gate 4 is very interesting. The quickest route is the 'High
Cross', involving a very advanced ferry glide close to the weir.
The difficulty, of course, is jumping on to the fast water, which
may be doing anything up to 30 m.p.h., and then off it again at
the other side. The expert will be adept at leaning to the downstream side to counteract the tendency for the fast water to

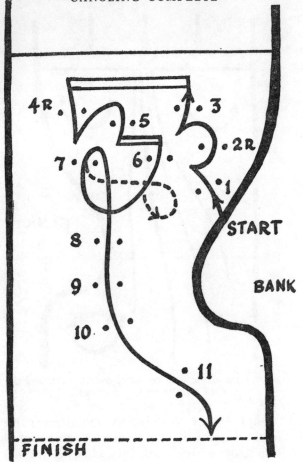

Fig. 23   An example of a suitable racing course

sweep the boat from under its occupant. For the less expert, a long paddle is indicated. A high telemark will be the safest way to enter gate 5, followed by a reverse ferry for gate 6.

There is a choice of routes to gate 7. The solid line shown may result in the boat being swept down a long way. As a precaution against this, an auxillary turn close to gate 2, which is now dead, could be made. This will keep the boat in the slower water for as long as possible. Gates 8, 9 and 10 look easy, but remember that the current is moving diagonally at this point.

Finally, a sting in the tail. As soon as the canoe gets between the poles of gate 11 it will be in the centre of an eddy and will promptly start turning. From here it is just a sprint to the end.

Skill and Stamina

So much for the rules of the game; but how to come out on top? As with any other competitive sport, fitness plays a very big part, and anyone expecting to succeed must be prepared to train hard.

First of all general stamina and 'wind' must be improved, with circuit training techniques, and then weight training should be used to develop the particular muscles required. But nothing can alter the fact that slalom is primarily a test of skill. Skill itself can be divided into technique and experience. The first of these can be perfected initially in the swimming pool and then on the river. The Eskimo roll is of vital importance to the slalomist. The popularity of rolling is attributed to the slalomists' desire to complete a run, but in reality its greatest virtue lies in its confidence-giving properties. As with any competition, the participant must know the limit of his capabilities and this can only be gained by constant practice.

For those who have no rough water near to home on which to practise, the Wiggle test is a very useful standby. If this is to be of value, your timekeeping friends must be very strict when watching for mistakes.

Slalom and Wild Water Racing Organization

Although the organization of individual events is handled by the clubs the overall management of both slalom and wild water racing is in the hands of the British Canoe Union Slalom Committee.

Full details of the fixture list, divisional system, entry arrangements and slalom organizing facilities can be obtained from the secretary, but individual coaching is better obtained via a local club. If there is no club in the immediate vicinity, canoeists can do much worse than contact either Chalfont Park C. C. if they live near to London or Manchester C. C. otherwise. The addresses of both these can be obtained from the BCU general secretary.

7

Racing: Sprint and Long Distance
MARIANNE TUCKER

THE two main branches in racing are sprint and long distance. Sprint is an Olympic event which was introduced into the Games in 1936 and is staged over set distances of 500, 1,000 and 10,000 metres, under the auspices of the International Canoe Federation. In Great Britain it is controlled by the Paddling Racing Committee of the British Canoe Union who are affiliated to the ICF. Long distance racing is a very popular pastime in this country but does not attract the same interest abroad, except for the Sella River Race in Spain and isolated events in Australia and America which bear little resemblance to long distance racing as we know it. It, too, is controlled by a Committee of the BCU. Courses can range in distance from 8 to 124 miles, the latter being the famous Devizes to Westminster Canoe Race inaugurated in 1949 and considered in some quarters as the forerunner to long distance racing as it is known today.

SPRINT RACING

Sprint racing may be considered the purest form of canoeing since it is a competition of speed in matched boats on static, or near static water. The word 'sprinting' is very misleading as medically and theoretically any event over 10 seconds in duration is no longer classed as a sprint, whereas canoe sprinting over the shortest official distance of 500 m. takes at least 1 min. 50 sec. for a world-class man and 2 min. 5 sec. for a world-class woman. Therefore, the word 'sprinting' is used in the broadest sense.

The starts in sprint are static and over 500 and 1,000 m. the course is straight and buoyed, with the competitors being not less than five metres apart and not more than nine in number

9. K4s racing on the Serpentine in London's Hyde Park. The annual Serpentine Regatta was last held in 1964 when the sponsors withdrew their support

10. The start of a K1 race at an international regatta at Zaandam, Holland

11. David Mitchell, British slalom champion, draws his boat sideways through the water as he approaches a gate

12. An excellent illustration of a canoeist leaning downstream on his paddle as he crosses fast water

in any heat. The water must have a minimum depth of six feet over the entire course so that no one competitor has unfair advantage over another.

The boats used in sprint racing are kayaks and Canadians. Dealing with the kayak first, the single is recognized by the notation K1 for a single, K2 for a double, and K4 for a kayak seating four persons. K-class boats are constructed of hot moulded veneer on the monocoque principle, i.e. frameless and without a keel. They are beautiful craft, sleek, but due to the design, rather unstable. The dimensional and weight limits are governed by the ICF and must conform to the following table given in metric units:

Type	Max. Length (in centimetres)	Min. Beam	Min. Weight (in kilograms)
K1	520	51	12
K2	650	55	18
K4	1100	60	30
C1	520	75	16
C2	650	75	20

As the subject of design is amply covered by Mr Samson in Chapter 1, I do not propose to dwell on it any further.

Canadian sprint racing is virtually non-existent in Britain. The last time we had a competitor in the Olympic Games was in 1952, when Gerald Marchand of Richmond Canoe Club represented Great Britain at Helsinki. However, this type of racing is extremely popular amongst the continental countries and there could be a revival of interest here with the recent introduction of a racing Canadian constructed of plywood on the chine principle.

C8s have been introduced from Germany and hold a lot of interest for clubs, youth organizations, schools, etc. These are 'home built' and can be paddled by complete novices, provided the steersman is an expert.

Paddles

There are two shapes available to paddlers, either the orthodox 'square' blade or the asymmetrical blade. Both are feathered to decrease wind resistance to the absolute minimum, and light, and manufactured with racing in mind—therefore, they will not stand up to too much harsh treatment.

It has been felt for a considerable time that there is room for a great deal of research into paddles. Recently, the asymmetrical shape was introduced initially by continental manufacturers, and experiments have shown that when the conventional blade enters the water the resistence is off centre and the blade has a tendency to twist, whereas with the asymmetrical shape the centre of pressure remains on the centre of the blade at all points of entry. Some work has been done on paddles in this country and findings indicate that it may be reasonable to expect that an efficient paddle will probably have most of the following features:

1. A laminated construction
2. Curved in a longitudinal direction
3. A shaped centre rib on front surface
4. An asymmetrical shape.

However, at this time many of the top-line paddlers are using the orthodox shape. Some have tried the asymmetrical paddle and have not been impressed with it. Probably this is a psychological problem partly due to prolonged use of the orthodox paddle and hence a resulting familiarity with it. But it would seem that a beginner is well advised to use the asymmetrical shape.

The length of the paddle is decided initially by standing, barefooted, with feet together and the paddle, with one end on the ground, held vertically in front of you. Stretch one arm fully in an upward direction and just curl the tips of the fingers over the top of the blade. I say, initially, as often once a paddler has become experienced he likes to experiment with different lengths until ultimately the ideal length for him is found. The width of grip on the loom is also very important and again, can be found by standing with paddle held horizontally in front of you with your hands on the loom so that you have a right angle at your elbow and also between your upper arm and the sides of your trunk. This gives the correct spacing for your hands. Some people use the same method but place the paddle on their heads. It has been found that if a piece of tape is put on the inside and outer limits of the grip it helps in keeping the hands in the right position when paddling. It is surprising how often you see a canoeist holding the paddles unevenly, the hands having slipped either to right or left.

Training to become a Sprint Paddler
To become a top-class paddler you need a K1 in good condition,

suitable paddles, a good technique and the right approach. The most important thing, in my opinion, is the right approach! You must want to win and mean to work hard enough to achieve this end. Positive thinking is the key and without it you might as well forget the idea of racing successfully. A good K1, the right paddles, and a good technique will get you so far but after that it is all in the mind. Having to train in adverse weather conditions, having to push past the point where your muscles are crying out for you to stop, having to stick to a disciplined routine—this is where your mind must take over and push you through.

Let us assume that you have the right mental approach and have obtained the K1 and paddles. The next essential is a good basic technique. The following method has not been devised by me but by continental coaches with years of practical experience behind them, and is now widely taught to beginners with great success. No two people appear to paddle the same, they all have natural limitations and characteristics, but the stroke can be broken down to what is the most effective way mechanically and it is up to the paddler and coach to try to achieve this end.

Technique

The basic principle of this technique is that the stroke does not start in the shoulders, but in the hips. The movement runs from the hip muscles over the back and chest to the shoulders and on to the upper forearm. The bodywork is supported by corresponding legwork, the opposite leg to the pushing hand being stretched in rhythm with the stroke, the foot pressed against the footrest. This movement is widely known as the 'cycling' action of the legs.

Sit upright, or lean very slightly forward in the boat, not too far or this will impede abdominal movement and breathing, and do not look into the cockpit or to the bow as this will tend to endanger the straight running of the boat. Look in the direction in which you are travelling. The legs are bent with closed knees and the steering bar held between the feet with the balls of the foot placed on the footbar and the heels resting together on the floor of the boat. Do not press the knees against the sides of the canoe, which is a common and erroneous method when first paddling a K-class boat, as it gives a false sense of stability. In fact, the legs cannot be used correctly and the transfer of effort through the knees into the cockpit will have a tipping effect on the boat.

To describe the movement of the paddle through air and water I will work systematically by giving the stroke on one side of the body. The work of the body starts by moving the hip forward, i.e. in the direction of the first stroke. Simultaneously with this movement, the hand brings the paddle forward at eye level, the back of the hand forming one line with the fore-arm (wrist straight), and in a straight line in the direction of the gunwale. Do not move the hand in the direction of the centre line of the boat, or across it, as this will upset the smooth running of the craft, which is all-important. The less dipping and rolling movements transferred to the boat the smoother and, therefore, faster it will travel. During the pushing phase of the movement the loom of the paddle is not gripped too tightly but rather sits in the crutch between the thumb and fore-finger with the fingers extended. Similarly, during the pulling phase the loom is gripped firmly to prevent water slipping away from the blade area and to transfer the power. This 'milking' action of gripping and relaxing the fingers allows fresh oxygen and blood to get to the muscles, which is essential, otherwise the cramped action of holding the muscles static for a period of time will, in due course, lead to strained forearm muscles and possibly to Teno-Synovitis, a common complaint to beginners.

When the arm is straight and the trunk fully rotated, bring the forward hand with the paddle straight down. Just before the blade dips into the water, turn it by a quick 90 degree flick of the wrist of the other hand, i.e. feather the blade to present it vertically to the water. Now we have come to the most important part of the whole movement—the pulling phase. Make certain that the arm is straight and the body is still fully rotated in a forward direction, then the blade must be dipped smoothly into the water just outside the wave which runs from bow to stern. If the paddle enters too closely to the boat, the paddle tends to curve in the first and last quarter of the stroke which causes the craft to veer off course resulting in a loss of speed. The first third of the stroke when the blade enters the water, and is pulled in a straight line backwards through the vertical position, is the most important part so it is essential that the blade is introduced into the water as far forward of the cockpit as possible. It is then carried backwards with a powerful pulling movement from the hip and shoulder muscles. The stroke ends level with the hip. After it has passed this point the blade is in an inefficient position mechanically and also has a braking effect on the speed of the boat.

The lifting of the blade from the water is effected by the other side of the body being rotated, keeping the arm straight and shoulder dropped in preparation for the commencement of the pulling phase on that side. The length of time spent with

Fig. 24   The paddle cycle

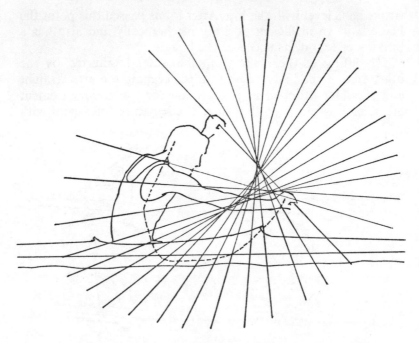

Fig. 25 Superimposed outline of the paddle cycle. The broken line indicates the path of the hand during the 'pulling' phase of the stroke

the blade out of the water must be kept to an absolute minimum as no propulsive effort can be applied (Figs. 24 & 25).

TRAINING SCHEDULE

The next step is to adopt an efficient training schedule for the year. This is broken down into three interlinked periods, namely, winter training, pre-racing training, racing training.

Keep an accurate record at all times of the work you have done, how you feel, morning pulse rate, weight, results and times achieved, etc. This can be a very useful guide in the future as to what sort of training achieves the best results, what period is necessary for obtaining peak condition, how you have progressed over the year, and can also convey a great deal of relevant information to a coach or doctor. The morning pulse rate should be taken before doing anything else. Keep a watch by the side of the bed. The pulse rate will indicate your state of fitness as the lower it is the fitter you are becoming. A loss in weight can indicate that the training is too harsh, especially if it is a sudden drop in weight, or it could suggest that a medical check-up is advisable. Obviously, everybody has a gradual loss in weight during the paddling season but most people find that this levels off at their 'racing weight'. Many paddlers like to have a medical check-up at the beginning of the season and I think it is a good idea as it gives you a psychological up-lift when the doctor passes you A1. He might suggest certain vitamins for you to take during an intensive schedule such as Vitamins E and C, and an iron supplement can be added to the diet.

To understand your training and why you do certain things it is as well to have a basic knowledge of how your body works. As canoeists, our primary concern is the conditioning to maximum efficiency of the trunk rotators, shoulder and arm muscles. A simple outline of muscle physiology and its relationship to the other body systems may help in understanding how this end is achieved; you should study one of the numerous books which have been written on this subject.

WINTER TRAINING—OCTOBER TO MARCH
General fitness can be obtained by running, swimming, games, gymnastics, free-standing exercises, etc. Running improves your cardio-vascular system and the coronary circulation improves enormously which is very important to alleviate coronary thrombosis in later life. If training is done for a long time the heart, in fact, enlarges and it is not a bad thing to have an enlarged heart. Providing there is no disease in the heart it is almost impossible to damage it. When running it is not a case of just going out and jogging along; one must work hard at it as you would at weight training, or paddling. One schedule that is advocated to start at the beginning of December should consist of the following, five nights a week:

$\frac{1}{4}$ mile run slowly—followed by—100 yd. flat out

followed by $\frac{1}{4}$ mile fast x 8.

This to be terminated at the end of March followed by one such session per week. Running up hills interspersed with suitable exercises is favoured by some. But it is a fact that running is an extremely important part of winter training and it should be *hard* running.

Swimming can be performed one night per week as this helps to relax the muscles. The session should consist of hard varied swimming and not just fooling around in the water.

Concentrate on front crawl, back crawl and butterfly, as these three strokes use similar muscles to canoeing. Try to have a game of football or basketball once a week. Gymnastics are excellent but here the skill level could be the limiting factor. Free-standing exercises help to loosen up the body and are valuable in getting the body warmed through before attempting weight or circuit training, or even paddling on a cold day. On the continent, skiing is an important part of winter training as the downward thrust has marked similarity to the pulling phase of the canoeing stroke; however, except in Scotland, there are few British paddlers who have a chance of enjoying this pastime.

Introduce as much variation as possible into your winter training. There is plenty of enforced routine training in the summer when it is difficult to introduce a lot of variety but in the winter there are many ways of getting fit that are good fun as well.

Once basic fitness has been obtained you should progress to training at a more intensive level, and it is now accepted that the use of weights is a most valuable part of an athlete's training. It was first introduced in 1936 by the Germans who used it in the preparation of their Olympic team.

Strength and power are best obtained by using heavy weights with low repetitions and endurance and stamina is best obtained by using light weights, or body weight, with a high number of repetitions. An ideal schedule is to start with weight training and then progress to circuit training.

Strength is the ability to produce force, and power is the ability to produce force continually. You must work at maximal, or near maximal, level to improve strength with few repetitions.

The generally accepted number of days per week for weight training is three, i.e. Monday, Wednesday and Friday. Sessions should be arranged so that you have a day's recovery in between. You may find at first that you feel very stiff on days following training but there is no reason to miss a session.

Keep a log of your progress, recording at each session exactly what you have done—this will give you the necessary information for the next session. Do not rely on your memory as it is unlikely that you will be able to remember the poundage used for each exercise and your log will also show you how you are progressing and give you information as to when you should change or adjust your schedule.

If you are a beginner, you would be well advised to join a

weightlifting club where you can get expert guidance and also have the use of good apparatus, or at least train with people who have more experience than yourself. Never try to lift heavy weights by yourself, otherwise, if you get into difficulties, there is nobody to help you. I remember once becoming caught under the bar whilst doing Bench Press and I had to yell the house down before somebody came to my aid, and I realized what a silly thing I had done. Technique is an integral part of weight training and this is something that cannot be learnt efficiently from books: you have to be shown and coached.

The racing canoeist uses the upper body and trunk, therefore a schedule should be devised that caters mainly for these muscles. The legs are not so important and they are covered to some extent by running. From the following list of exercises a schedule can be built up:

Squats
Bench Press
Straight Arm Pullovers
Upright Rowing
Bent-over Rowing
Rotation Sit-ups
Lateral Raise
Military Press
Wrist Rolling
Single Arm Rowing

There are other exercises which can be used but the ones mentioned above are the ones most widely used by canoeists. When working out a schedule, take six exercises and arrange them so that you are not using the same muscle groups consecutively. For instance, Bench Press, Straight Arm Pullover, Rotation Sit-ups, Wrist Rolling—these exercises are not using the same muscles.

At the beginning of the strength training season have an introductory period of two to three weeks, assuming training is being done on three evenings per week. Relatively light weights will be used at first and attention can be given to technique. Working poundages must be assessed initially by trial and error; if the poundage is correct you will only just be able to complete the last repetition in your final set.

As with all methods of training there are various ideas on how a schedule should be constructed and I will mention several methods.

(*a*) Three sets of six repetitions. After each set you should have a reasonable rest. If you are training in a group of three, do the exercises in strict rotation and you will find that this gives ample rest.

(*b*) Four sets of three repetitions in each exercise.

(*c*) Five sets of two repetitions in each exercise. A suggested progression from this would be:

(*d*) A pyramid set consisting of four, three, two and one repetition in each exercise.

(*e*) A pyramid set consisting of eight, six, four repetitions at one weight, say 75 lb., and then three, two, one repetitions starting at three at 70 lb., then two at 75 lb., and finally one at 80 lb.

An experienced weightlifting coach will be able to gauge your abilities and will suggest what method to adopt.

Once you are able to do one more repetition after what should be your last repetition, the working poundage should be increased. Generally speaking, the larger the muscle groups which are being used, the greater will be the increase. As the weights get heavier you will need a longer recovery period between each set.

It has been suggested that the introduction of 'Olympic' lifts into a weight training programme will be an asset in the development of power. However, because of the speed of the movement a greater degree of technique is required with these exercises:

Power Cleans
Clean and Jerk
Power Squats
Snatching

Paddling at this period of training takes a minor role. Some top paddlers do not paddle at all and, if the winter is a severe one, many stretches of water are iced over. If you do wish to paddle during the winter, concentrate on your technique and build up mileage. Always try to paddle in a group just in case you get into trouble or capsize. Wear suitable clothing—there is no need to go out bundled up but rather wear a long-sleeved woollen jumper, an anorak which is windproof and a tracksuit. If you have particular trouble with cold legs a pair of tights helps to keep you warm, and I have found that wet boots taken from a wet suit used in diving and water skiing have solved the problem of cold feet. With the use of a spray deck you should be very warm. Unfortunately, your hands will suffer with the cold. You can rub the backs with grease, making sure you do not get it on the inside of your hands, but do not wear gloves. Actually, your warming-up exercises before getting onto the water will help to warm them up.

PRE-SEASON TRAINING: MARCH TO MAY

At the end of February a circuit can be introduced on the second evening of weight training so that you would be doing a weight session, a circuit and another weight session. As I mentioned earlier there must be a progression throughout your whole year's training.

Circuit training, where you have a high number of repetitions and low weights, or body weight, will not make you as strong as weight training but it will improve endurance. It improves both the circulation and the efficiency of the muscles to contend with extended exercise. You may have heard the expression, 'local endurance': this means that the muscle groups used in paddling must be trained in such a way that they can work for long periods without feeling fatigued. You will probably have found during a race that your arms feel like dropping off and that is the limiting factor, not your breathing. There are numerous ways in which this can be overcome but probably the most convenient way is with circuit training.

This form of training is no more than a series of consecutive exercises which are done in rapid succession. You can have circuits without any form of apparatus or more sophisticated ones using weights and gym apparatus. Again, if possible, consult an experienced person in this field who can devise a circuit to cover your particular facilities.

Try to train in a group as the element of competition helps enormously. Do not take a rest between exercises or circuits, but run between each exercise for, in order to gain full value, everything must be done as quickly as possible. If somebody is doing the exercise which you want to do next, do not wait for them to finish but rather do another one. Endeavour to work your circuit so that you are not doing exercises which involve the same muscle groups in succession. Do not cheat in the way you do the exercises or in the number of repetitions—you are only cheating yourself. If you have decided to do the circuits against a watch, do not let the quality of the exercises drop just to achieve a faster completion time.

When doing this form of training it is easy to forget the number of repetitions for each exercise and a useful tip is to write them on a piece of paper or cardboard, placed in position where a number of people working at the same time at different exercises will not interfere with each other. In group training it is desirable to have three grades of circuit so that people of varying ability are catered for, i.e. A, B and C, A being the hardest one with the highest number of repetitions.

Always become completely familiar with the circuit and make sure that you are doing each exercise properly. As your degree of efficiency improves, move to a higher circuit until you are doing three As. Remember that if you are using weights they should be heavy enough to make you work hard but not so large that they stop you from doing the exercises very rapidly. At the end of March the weight training session can be dropped completely and the circuits increased to two periods per week with two days rest in between.

As you can see, there is now a progression from weight to circuits and paddling. Water work cannot be done in many cases in the evenings early in the year but use should be made of the weekends. Cover mileage, paying particular attention to technique, and try and iron out any faults you may have. Ask an experienced person to watch you, as it is impossible to see how you are paddling yourself unless you are able to have a cine film made. I would recommend you to have a cine loop taken if possible, as it is very difficult at times to visualize your own faults even if told by somebody else. When the lighter evenings arrive, start paddling once or twice during the week.

RACING TRAINING

As you might expect, there are many conflicting ideas on training but the basis of them all is hard work. I feel that if you are prepared to work hard and sincerely believe in the type of work you are doing, then you can achieve results. It is very important to have a working programme which is aimed at bringing you to peak condition for the major events. Prepare a weekly schedule that fits in with the overall plan, otherwise you may go onto the water without any definite ideas and tend to waste time. Record in your log each day exactly what you have done that evening.

Of course we are not all able to train on ideal water conditions or have the same amount of time available for training, or be training for the same distances, so I would certainly not lay down any hard-and-fast rules as to types of training, particularly when what would suit one person would not do for another. Remember, a schedule must be an individual thing: a general plan could be given to a group but it must be then tailored to suit individual needs.

Because of your winter training you are now capable of facing the demands of the coming racing season with confidence. You should be feeling fit and well and awaiting eagerly the first race of the year.

Ideally your training will be covering six nights a week with one rest day. To fit this in with the racing programme, Friday should be the rest day as most regattas are held on Saturday. Your programme can be broken down into three light sessions and three heavy sessions, i.e. Monday, Wednesday and Sunday, light sessions and Tuesday, Thursday and Saturday heavy sessions. This does not mean that during the light sessions you do not work hard but rather that you vary the intensity of your programme. A light circuit can be included twice a week in your schedule.

At all times use a stopwatch when training, especially on tidal waters where it is difficult to get accurate distances due to variation in water flow. It is then possible to build up a schedule using lengths of time for sprinting rather than actual distances. For instance, a set of five 2-minute sprints at 70 per cent effort, with a recovery period of 1 minute between each sprint, the set being repeated twice with a 5-minute easy paddle between each set. Another alternative is a pyramid of five 1½-minute sprints with 1-minute recovery periods between each sprint, followed by a 5-minute easy paddle, then four 1-minute sprints, three 30-second sprints, two 20-second sprints, the sprints being separated by suitable recovery periods. Or five 1½-minute sprints, four 2-minute sprints, three 2½-minute springs, two 3-minute sprints, one 4-minute sprint. The latter being particularly beneficial to 1,000 m. paddlers. Many combinations can be worked out in this manner.

The length of recovery between each sprint is, again, a question of individual fitness and one way of gauging this is taking your pulse after a sprint. Having finished your first sprint, paddle gently for one minute and then take your quarter-minute pulse. This should be 30 or less if you are reasonably fit. If over 30, rest for another half-minute and check your quarter-minute pulse again. It is almost certain that your minute pulse is now down to 120. As soon as the minute pulse is down to 120 you are ready to start work again. Eventually you will find that you will reach the 120 mark inside one minute. It is not necessary to take your pulse after every sprint but take it after the first and second burst of the first set and then work out your recovery period accordingly.

Practise starts constantly, and try and arrange a time trial once a week over an accurately measured course. A time trial over the same stretch of water will give an indication of your progress throughout the season and will also provide valuable experience of paddling over the actual distance that will be raced. For some it may mean travelling a distance to find a suitable course but the effort is well worth while.

During the first few weeks of racing training it is advisable not to try and sprint at 100 per cent effort as your muscles are not ready for a maximum load. Concentrate on build-ups, technique and generally becoming familiar with sprinting. Fartlek training is particularly good at this time of the year where the paddler just sprints for as long as he wishes with no controlled recovery period between each burst. If possible, train in a group where the element of competition is heightened and any one paddler can take the initiative by trying to paddle away from the group.

Before an important competition allow a period for tapering off your training. I would suggest that approximately ten days before the race you start to shorten the length of your sprints and the intensity of your schedule, until four days before the event you are just doing two sets of 30-second or 20-second bursts. On the third day before the event, have an easy paddle and then take two days off. This should allow you to be fully rested and tuned for the event.

Race Preparation

The end to which all your hard work has been aimed is now in sight. You know your own capabilities and are prepared physically and mentally for the race.

On the day of the event the most important thing is not to become flustered by the hustle and bustle. Check on the times of your events, whether there are heats, semi-finals and finals, and plan your day and meals accordingly. Arrive at the venue in plenty of time and make certain that there have been no alterations to the programme. If it is possible to check the course, do so; this is particularly useful in long-distance racing when portaging is involved.

Inspect your boat and paddles thoroughly, making certain that everything is secured properly and in the right position; there is nothing worse than having to retire from a race because the steering has gone wrong, or the footrest has come loose. Also check your start number with the officials and, if possible, collect it so that it can be fixed to the boat in plenty of time.

Change into racing kit with time to spare and carry out your warming-up preparations. Some people prefer to warm up twenty minutes before their event and then paddle straight to the start. However, many of the top paddlers are now using the following method of warm-up. One hour and ten minutes before their event they get boated and proceed with warming up for fifteen minutes and then do either a flat out 500 m. for a 1,000 m. race, or 250 m. flat out for a 500 m. race, finishing with a gentle paddle back to the starting point so that the warm-up is finished fifty minutes before the start of the event. If you use this method, wrap up warmly in a tracksuit, etc., after finishing and find somewhere to relax until you are called for your race.

Keep within the range of the Starter's call at the time of the start and paddle around gently until you are called up. Once in your starting position, keep relaxed and control your breathing. If you are on a held start you will have no problem keeping the boat on station, but if you are not held just keep it in position with gentle sculling strokes. Do not be caught napping on the start, listen carefully to what the Starter is saying and have your paddle in the correct position for the word 'Go'.

At the finish do not hang about but rather don a warm tracksuit, or get dressed if you have no more races that day.

10,000-Metre Events
A 10,000 m. event is conducted in a different way to 500 m. and 1,000 m. events. Both tactics and wash hanging come into play and it is necessary for a 10,000 m. paddler to be familiar with these.

Tactics depend entirely on who is in the race and knowing the weak and strong points of your opponents. You have to judge when it is a good moment to try and break away from the bunch, or when to overtake. This will come with experience.

Your tactics have to be decided *before* the race, if possible, so that you have a definite picture of what you intend to do. At all times your moves must be fair. It is not gamesmanship to lose your opponent on a buoy or any similar obstruction when you think there is nobody watching, but it is fair to paddle him off by sprinting away at an angle and then returning to your normal course so causing him to lose your wash.

Wash hanging is permitted up to the last 1,000 m. of a 10,000 m. event and should be practised in training as any paddler will find it a most useful attribute. It is achieved by placing your bow level with the cockpit of another boat so that you are sitting on the bow wave of the other craft. The canoes should be approximately three feet apart. The psychological effect on your opponent is to your advantage but, in fact, he is not slowed down by you sitting on his wash, and he could have the advantage on bends.

LONG-DISTANCE RACING

This branch of competitive canoeing is extremely popular in this country, and is a challenge which has caught many canoeists' imagination. At some events there are over 200 competitors and the numbers are increasing each year. It is controlled by the Long Distance Racing Committee. At one time events were held under a handicap system, the most well known being the C. N. Davies formula; but today canoes are divided into classes depending on their specifications. L. D. racing has taken tremendous strides forward because British manufacturers have specialized in canoes for this form of racing which they can supply either complete ex-works, or in kit form. Some of the classes are suitable for light touring and the NCK1 is a good sea boat. The paddles are the same as for sprint racing but the L.D. rules stipulate that buoyancy is compulsory for national ranking races and that lifejackets should be carried.

The classes are as follows:—

Class 1—Kayaks within K1 specification. Open class.

Class 2a Seniors and 2b Juniors—National chine kayak single.

Class 3a Seniors, 3b Juniors, 3c Ladies—Hard-skinned single kayaks with a maximum L.O.A. of 15 ft and a minimum beam of 23 in.

Class 4a Seniors, 4b Juniors, 4c Ladies—Rigid and folding

soft-skinned single-seater kayaks with a maximum L.O.A. of 15 ft and a minimum beam of 23 in.

Class 5 Open double—Kayaks with the K2 specification.

Class 6a Seniors, 6b Juniors, 6c Ladies—Rigid and folding soft-skinned double kayaks with a maximum L.O.A. of 17 ft 6 in. and a minimum beam of 27 in.

Class 7a Seniors, 7b Juniors, 7c Ladies—Hard-skinned double kayaks with a maximum L.O.A. of 17 ft and a minimum beam of 27 in.

These classes are subject to alteration if deemed necessary by the Long Distance Racing Committee.

I have covered paddling technique in the previous section on sprint racing and the same technique should be used in long-distance racing events as it is the most efficient way of paddling. I have also covered training but would point out that this would vary on distance on the water as it would be useless to train over a 500 m. stretch for a race covering up to fifteen miles. A schedule should be worked out in the same manner, remembering that a L.D. event can be held as early as February.

The Long Distance Racing National Coach has produced a booklet entitled *Long Distance Racing Handbook*, published by the British Canoe Union, which sets out a suggested schedule for training for L.D. races and provides other useful information.

The ability to handle your craft in all conditions is an essential part of this form of racing. Each course varies: one week you can be paddling on the sea, and the next paddling on a winding narrow stream, or shooting rapids; in fact, you can encounter various conditions in a single event. As mentioned in the sprint section, wash hanging and tactics are another part of L.D. racing and if you become adept at these particular arts it is another step towards winning a race.

Portaging becomes easier with practice, so try portaging in training, paying particular attention to team work if you are paddling a double. Become familiar with getting in and out at different places, carrying your boat in a comfortable position and making sure you do not lose contact with your paddle. Races can be won or lost at a portage as the vital seconds can be wasted through doing it badly. If you can inspect the portages at a course before the race, do so—picking out where you will land and get afloat again and taking note of any particular hazards.

As with sprint racing, arrive at the venue in plenty of time and make certain there have been no alterations to start times. Some events are well organized and there are plenty of marshals to make certain that you do not take a wrong turn on the course, but on occasion the organization is not quite so good, so always try to memorize the course and whether you are able to land at a portage on the left- or right-hand side. Also make a note as to whether weirs are shootable or have to be portaged.

Long-distance racing can be really good fun. Although many paddlers train seriously for this type of racing, it is not quite so arduous as sprinting as there is also an element of luck and, to a certain extent, an element of battling with the varying conditions as well as with your opponents.

Having read this chapter on sprint racing and long-distance racing you might ask what is achieved by all this hard work. It is a challenge, it is character building, it develops your mental as well as physical abilities, and the long-term effects of disciplined training and having a healthy body will show in later life.

8

Safety in Canoeing

OLIVER COCK

SOME time ago the Metropolitan Police put out a plea that, should any member of the public see anything untoward happening, or a policeman struggling with a malefactor, he should at once do all he could to stop the malefactor and assist the police. One of the societies which attempts to prevent injury through accident let it be known that they were opposed to this plea by the police; they opined that the public should not go to the assistance of a policeman in difficulties. It is good to know that the public shortly afterwards took the opportunity to show they disagreed with the society's recommendations by coming very much to the assistance of the police in the case of an armed man in a stolen car.

But was the society's recommendation to be safe the right one or not? Is there any way to be certainly safe in life? Is it not better to meet the danger, to be prepared for it and to know what to do when it happens, *before it happens*?

This chapter heading may have the same effect on some readers as the police plea did on the society—'If canoeing is dangerous—better not canoe'. But this attitude is a negative one. If it is carried into life it produces no progress, and no progress is progress backwards when viewed by those who are going forwards. The second attitude is surely the better one: if there are dangers ahead, let us find out what these dangers are; let us learn how to deal with them; and then, when they appear, we shall know what to do, and the situation will quickly come under control.

All adventurous activities necessarily have a modicum of danger about them, otherwise they would not be adventurous. Come to that, some of the less adventurous activities contain an element of risk—even at cricket one may be hit and injured by a flying ball. When one comes to deal with activities which involve the elements, or physical features of the countryside, these risks are greatly increased. Thus in gliding, immense care is taken to ensure that the glider is in perfect condition; in rock climbing, every precaution is taken against falls. What should one do when one comes upon an activity dealing with water?

Whichever of the elements one is dealing with, the important thing is to learn something about it. You cannot glide without knowing which way the wind is blowing. You do not wisely climb on crumbling rock. Equally, with any given piece of water, you should discover what is likely to happen when you get involved with it.

There are a number of ways one can enjoy oneself on the water, but, whatever one is going to do, the first law of safety is:

LEARN TO SWIM

And by swimming is not meant just a pleasant bathe in a warm swimming pool, with people around to pull you out if necessary, but in an ice-cold river, or in a lake, or at sea with the waves buffeting you. Can you swim there? Are you happy there? If you are, you are likely to be safe.

But why all this fuss about swimming? *You* are going canoeing. *You* have no intention of going swimming! We agree; but every enthusiastic canoeist has found himself swimming at some time or other. It is the unexpectedness of it which makes it dangerous. If you are ready for the swim, then there is nothing dangerous in it. Therefore the next item on the agenda to make you safe is practising swimming from your canoe. What is it like suddenly to be flung into the water? What is it like if your canoe fills with water and founders? What is it like suddenly to be turned upside down under it? Can you get out? How do you get out? Well, better to choose a time and a place where it is reasonably comfortable, and where you can organize some friends to come to your help if necessary. If you don't like it the first time, do it again and again until you begin to enjoy it—and, we promise you, in time you will. And when you enjoy it, you will be safe.

Perhaps we had better look at this capsizing game more closely, because there are rules which will ensure your always being able to get out of your canoe if you obey them. Here is how to do it, then, when you are learning in your comfortable surroundings, with your friends around to help if necessary.

CAPSIZE DRILL

First of all, make quite certain that you are alone in your cockpit—that is, that you are not sharing it with loose ends of rope, or bags of equipment, or *anything else whatever*. There is no surer way of getting jammed in your canoe when you capsize than by being slack about this point.

Now proceed as follows:

1. Put your paddle beside you, floating on the water.

2. Lean forward and grasp the gunwales as far forward as you can reach. You are now looking into the cockpit or at the deck of your canoe. You must remain looking that way until you are entirely clear of the canoe, underneath it.

3. Capsize.

4. Remain looking into the cockpit or at the deck, release your grasp of the gunwales.

5. If you have a spray cover on, release this, either from the cockpit coaming, or from yourself if it is the type that is fixed to the canoe.

6. Still looking into the cockpit or at the deck, put your hands beside your hips, on the side of your canoe, and push yourself out. Be sure not to kick with your legs—let them slide smoothly out of the cockpit. Aim to go downwards as you leave the canoe—this will ensure the clean exit of your body and legs. Too hasty an attempt to break the surface may mean that you will get stuck in the cockpit. It will also allow air to escape from the upturned canoe.

7. When you are clear of the canoe, swim to the surface, collect your paddle if you can, swim to one end of the canoe and hold it. Don't otherwise interfere with it. Neither try to right it, nor roll it over, nor climb onto it. By all these means you will waterlog your canoe and lose a life raft.

8. Swim to the side, towing or pushing your canoe, swimming how you like.

9. At the side empty it, or get your friends to help you empty it, and carry on.

With practice, this drill will become a habit, and when you capsize accidentally you will easily be able to cope with the situation. You will be safe.

PREPARING FOR THE UNEXPECTED

Now let us look at the Second Law of Safety. This is a very

common law of life, well known yet seldom recognized until it is too late. It is the law which allows the unexpected always to happen. Usually known as the Eternal Law of Cussedness, it is also sometimes called Fingle's Law. There seems no reason for this, but that is the way of the Eternal Law of Cussedness, and Mr Fingle—whoever he may have been—is a very good friend, to be kept up your sleeve.

The truth is that canoeing is enormous fun. If you are continually expecting the unexpected to happen, then it isn't unexpected, is it? If you are prepared for the unexpected to happen, then, when it does happen you are not frightened by it and all is well. The dangerous factor—the killing factor—in all this is being unprepared, and consequently panicking. When a person panics, all collected, coherent thought leaves him. He is useless, powerless, and a menace to any who come to his help.

If Fingle's Law dogs one through life anyway, it certainly dogs a canoeist's life. Because the permutations and combinations of unexpectedness are infinite, it would take more than a lifetime for one to be fully prepared for all eventualities. A list of all the things that might happen would be infinite, too; but experience has shown that some things occur more often than others. We have already dealt with two of them, swimming and capsizing. Let us make a short list of the other things one should or should not do (Fig. 26).

In our list of 'do's and don't's', why are these chosen as most important to canoeists? We have already dealt with some, so we will not mention these again.

Buoyancy
Buoyancy prevents you and your canoe from sinking. Buoyancy for the canoe is easy, so long as you use common sense. It means bags of air held in the canoe, so that when the canoe fills with water it doesn't sink. Anything that holds air and does not leak will do. Even your clothes packed into a waterproof bag hold enough air to keep the canoe afloat. Distribute the air bags in the canoe so that, even when it is full of water, it will float on an even keel, and make them secure. We have seen a man who had put buoyancy into one end of his canoe only, trying to rescue something which looked like Cleopatra's Needle as it floated off downstream. We have also seen a canoe sink to the bottom of the river with two airbags left floating wistfully on the surface to mark the point of its descent!

DO's and DON'T's for CANOEISTS !!!

DON'T canoe if you cannot swim

DO provide buoyancy: always air bags in your boat, and a life-jacket for yourself where a capsize would be dangerous—in the sea, heavy rapids, floods, and cold water.

DO ask about local conditions: tides, currents, rapids, and weather changes can all be dangerous.

DON'T go out alone without having told someone where you are going and how long you think you will be.

DON'T put more people in a canoe than it is designed to carry.

DON'T wear wellingtons. You cannot swim in heavy boots.

DON'T change places

DO keep clear of of other craft.

DO keep away from weirs. They are dangerous.

DON'T right a capsized canoe. Hang on to it. It will float and you may not.

DON'T be put off by this list. It is all common sense really.

DO **REMEMBER** —better safe than sorry.

DO learn to canoe properly, and take the B.C.U. Tests

Fig. 26

The Life-jacket

Personal buoyancy is a much more complex affair, and a very great deal has been written and discovered recently about life-saving equipment. It all started when the Consumers' Association and the British Standards Institution discovered themselves both investigating the position in 1962. The Consumer's Association issued a report through their journal *Which?* showing that there were very few life-*saving* jackets at all, but a great many jackets on the market purporting to be life-saving jackets which in fact bordered on being murderous.

After much experimentation, and assistance from the Royal Navy and others, some of the features of a life-saving jacket are now becoming known and understood. There is much more to learn, but the British Standards Institution has published a standard with which all life-jackets should comply.

Besides quality of material, which is of course vital, but which need not bother you as a purchaser, provided the jacket has the BSI kite mark on it, what are the important features of a life-jacket?

(*a*) The life-jacket must be satisfactory under the worst possible conditions, that is to say, supporting an unconscious person in rough water.

(*b*) It must under no circumstances slip off over the head.

(*c*) Vital nerves leave the head via the back and side of the neck, and these must be kept as warm as possible. Therefore the jacket must fit even more snugly round the neck.

(*d*) In order that the patient's face be kept as far out of the water as possible, the buoyancy of the jacket must support him round the neck, tilting him backwards at an angle of approximately 45 degrees, leaving his legs to dangle as they will.

(*e*) *At least* 35 lb. of buoyancy are required to accelerate a body which has just slid down one wave to going up the next. Less buoyancy will mean that his head may go *through* the next wave instead of *over* it.

(*f*) Since the patient is slung on his back at an angle of 45 degrees, there will be a larger proportion of buoyancy in front of than behind him. This means that, should he have his back to the oncoming waves, his head will pass through them before the buoyancy has had a chance to lift him up over them. Therefore the jacket must contrive to turn him round quickly, to face into the oncoming waves. Due to the velocities of water within a wave, which cause the water to rise and fall as the wave progresses, 45 degrees was found also to be the correct angle at which the patient should be held in the water, to induce his automatically facing the waves.

The BSI also ruled that the jacket should put the patient into the right position in the water in a maximum of three seconds, without any effort on his part; that it should be easy to put on in half a minute; that it should be fitted with a life-line by which the patient could secure himself to his boat or to others in the water; that it should be equipped with a plastic whistle, so that he could draw attention to himself without taking the skin off his lips; and that it should be fitted with a lifting becket, so that rescuers could gct him easily out of the water.

So much, then, for the general characteristics of a life-saving jacket; but there are some which are peculiar to canoeists. Canoeing is a hot recreation, so the jacket must be sufficiently ventilated to allow the sweat to evaporate. There must be no chafing of the arm or neck of the wearer. A capsize always occurs unexpectedly; therefore the jacket must be worn at all times; therefore it must be comfortable. In a capsize, buoyancy of as much as 35 lb. may push the canoeist up into his canoe and prevent him escaping from it; but he must have some buoyancy in his jacket to ensure his coming to the surface. A figure of approximately 20 lb. has been found to be satisfactory for this. Nevertheless he must be able easily to increase this buoyancy to the requisite 35 lb. whilst he is swimming, should he be in the water for any length of time.

These are not easy conditions to fulfil; but there are life-saving jackets which comply with these requirements, having an inherent buoyancy of 20 lb. which can be increased easily to 35 lb. either by oral inflation or by manually operated bottle, though the latter adds very considerably to the cost. Automatic inflation cannot be accepted, as this has to operate within three seconds, and this does not necessarily allow the canoeist time to escape from his upturned craft.

Life-saving jackets having the BSI kite mark cannot be cheap, but what are *you* worth? There are things on the market sold as life-jackets, which will drown you as easily as anything will. They cost five or ten shillings. Is this a wise economy?

Overloading

A canoe becomes grossly unstable if it is overloaded. A canoe designed to carry one person will be unsafe with two people in it. Besides, very often the cockpit is not big enough to allow two people in together. They have to get in one at a time, and get out the same way. That is all very well the right way up, but what about upside down?

Footwear
If you cannot swim in heavy boots, you certainly cannot swim in wellingtons. Besides which, the loose top rim of the wellington allows you to get into the canoe all right, but catches in the framework when you try to get out—especially when upside down and in a hurry. Do not, however, canoe in bare feet. Our rivers all too often contain broken bottles, tins, and other sharp objects—cut feet are always unpleasant and often go septic. Avoid them by wearing gym shoes.

Changing places
Have you ever tried changing places on a tandem bicycle without getting off first? A canoe is also a very tippy vehicle. If you want to change places, get to the bank or beach, and do it there.

Collisions
A canoe is not only tippy, it is light and frail. If you take on any other vessel, you are going to be the loser. Therefore just get out of the way. Remember, too, that you may well not be visible to a larger craft. If you are ever run down by a power-driven boat, you will be very lucky if you escape very severe injury from the propellor blades.

Weirs
Take it that weirs are dangerous. You will see photographs and films of experts shooting them, and playing about below them, but they are experts. They know what they are doing, and they have learnt to interpret the movements of the water until they can judge what is safe and what is dangerous. Very often a weir that looks safe to shoot is more dangerous than one that looks dangerous. Only tackle a weir when accompanied by an experienced canoeist.

Distress Flares
This is another item which it is essential to have with you if you are going into open waters such as the sea, estuaries or large lakes. Here again the Consumers' Association has issued a report, and again the peculiar requirements of the canoeist must be borne in mind before rushing out to buy.

The flare is going to be operated at water level, most probably *in* the water. Therefore it must be waterproof, even to the extent of operating under the water for a few seconds. Because you may be under a cliff and the people whose attention you want to attract are back from the edge of the cliff, the flare must throw a signal high into the sky. To be carried conveniently in a canoe it must be small. Smoke disperses too quickly in a high wind and may be missed. The best flare therefore is a bright red one, lasting a minute if possible, during which time it will throw red stars into the sky. Quite small and economic flares which do all this are available from ships' chandlers, and every sea canoeist should have some.

Crash Helmets

Occasionally you will see canoeists shooting rapids, wearing crash helmets. The canoeists are usually experts and the rapids dangerous. Their precaution is a wise one since a capsize might result in the canoeist hitting his head on a rock and knocking himself out. Special helmets are made for canoeists which allow the water to drain out immediately. It is rather a specialized piece of equipment and one which does not usually concern the ordinary canoeist.

KEEP YOUR EQUIPMENT IN GOOD ORDER

We have so far been dealing with equipment which is special to emergencies. But it is equally important that all equipment should be in good working order. We are reminded of the incident of the small boy who was heard to exclaim: 'Sir! Sir! This canoe doesn't function!' Whereupon he rolled slowly over, to reveal a hole through which 'Sir' could easily have pushed both fists together. It is only common sense that the hull itself be kept in functioning order before, during and after one goes afloat. A proper repair kit appropriate to your canoe must be carried.

Paddles

These must be well maintained and varnished—if a paddle breaks during a trip the canoeist is helpless; therefore many prudent canoeists carry a second paddle with them for just this emergency. If it is of a jointed variety, the joint should not be sloppy. If this does happen, soaking in water for some hours will usually swell the wood again and tighten it.

Spray Covers

These have become an important piece of equipment. Most

modern ones are designed to stay with the canoeist, rather than remain on the canoe. If yours is one of these, then it must be secure round the waist, otherwise it may slip down and hinder your swimming. Such spray covers must also easily come off the cockpit coaming, and a round cockpit is more likely to ensure this than an angular one. Besides, it is not easy to make corners really waterproof; and a leak, even on the deck, may lead you into trouble if the water is rough enough.

If the cover is designed to stay with the canoe, then it must stay there. It should not be able to break loose, even half way. And you must be able to escape clean away from it. A zip fastener looks very tidy, and usually zips satisfactorily. The time when it won't is when you are upside down and Fingle has got hold of it. Then how do you get out?

Painters

These cause more argument among canoeists than any other item of equipment. Obviously they must be sound, to prevent them letting you down. There must be provision for one at both ends of the canoe, otherwise you will find yourself always want-ing it at the end where you have not got it. However it is arranged, it should never have the chance to become loose while you are afloat, otherwise, somehow, it will tangle on you at the very moment you want to be free. There is even argument for doing it up into a hank and pushing it into the kangaroo pouch of your anarak, safely out of the way but immediately available when you want it.

Glass-fibre canoes, with their very slippery hulls, must have a small loop of line at the bow and stern, in order to give people something to hold them by.

It is no good your having perfect equipment if you don't know how to use it. Just as with a bicycle it is useless if you cannot balance it, so with a canoe you must have a sound basic technique. A few people pick this up naturally, without being taught or shown; but the easier way is to have lessons, when it will not be necessary to discover everything by trial and error. There are only a few basic skills in canoeing. When you have learnt these, and practised them until you can use them at the appropriate moment without wasting time thinking what you ought to do next, you will be well on your way to becoming a proficient and safe canoeist.

RESCUE METHODS

On the River

Having, as we hope, persuaded you that old Fingle is going to get hold of you at some time or other, however hard you try to avoid him, let us now turn to methods by which you may get yourself out of predicaments, and how you may also assist others out of theirs.

First, here are some suggestions about tours on rivers.

Like any other expedition, river trips must be properly prepared for. Not only must local knowledge be obtained, particularly with regard to the weather, fallen trees and other obstructions, but the BCU Guide to Waterways should be consulted if the expedition is in this country; if abroad, then consult the relevant national canoe association—the BCU will provide the necesssary details.

The minimum size of *any* canoeing party should be three. The ideal maximum size of a party is between six and eight. Any party which is larger should always be split into smaller groups. Before going on the river, everyone must know who is in charge, who is to go down first, and, most important of all, who is the last man. The leader of the expedition will not necessarily go first. In fact he is more likely to choose a reliable aide-de-camp and send him on ahead, whilst he remains right at the back, acting as 'Tail-End Charlie' to make sure that everyone in the party is safe. A whistle is extremely useful, and simple signals should be agreed upon.

The party should never become separated. Frequent pauses must be made—the leader will wait for 'Tail-end Charlie', whose arrival will guarantee that the party is complete.

In his chapter on slalom and white water canoeing, Julian Shaw gives some more advanced advice on the behaviour of rough water. For the average canoeist on the average British river, the following remarks will be helpful and probably sufficiently comprehensive:

In general, paddle firmly, above all when approaching and going through faster water. By doing this, you keep steerage way on your canoe and thus control over it. If you are swung broadside and right round by the current just before a rapid, it is far better to continue down backwards rather than run the risk of being caught in the broadside position, when you will inevitably hit an obstruction, almost certainly capsize and probably damage your canoe.

The water will always flow fastest through its deepest part: for this reason always canoe round the outside bend of a river. Aim your canoe at the fastest water in a rapid—the force of the water itself will keep you clear of most rocks.

OBSTACLES

There is an important difference between natural obstacles lying in the river—mainly rocks, large boulders, etc.—and obstacles hanging over the water or put there by man (overhanging trees, posts with barbed wire, general garbage, etc.). Keep clear of overhanging trees and other comparable obstacles which have no effect on the flow of the current, otherwise you will find yourself pinned against them and in a potentially dangerous situation. Tree trunks which have been uprooted and carried off downstream, and then wedged across a rapid, are particularly dangerous. This is another reason for always reconnoitring a rapid from the bank, however well you think you know it from previous trips.

The first confusion that most often arises is the sudden stopping of the canoe as it floats over an apparently unobstructed and smooth piece of water. You have found an underwater obstruction, which we hope will not be so sharp as to tear a hole in the bottom of your canoe. The most likely method of freeing the canoe is to retire again, by exactly the same route by which you had arrived. If this is impossible you may have to get out; but before you do this, feel down on both sides of the canoe, with your paddle or your hand, or look down, to see if the obstruction sticks out on one side or the other. If it does, step out on that side, as it cannot be more than a few inches deep, and you will only get your feet wet. Step out on the other side, and you may well disappear under water. This will amuse your friends, if not you. If the obstruction has holed your canoe, you are going to get wet anyway, so the quicker you get out the better. Then the canoe will rise quickly and you may be able to get it ashore before it gets too waterlogged.

Sometimes, when the river is flowing fast, the canoe will be slewed round sideways against the rock it has hit, and have the whole pressure of the current press it against the rock. On no account allow the canoe to tip over upstream, so that the water may flow into the cockpit. Press hard on the downstream gunwale and get out as quickly as you can. If you get out on the downstream side of the canoe, be careful that the sudden lightening of it does not free it and let it knock you off your feet. If you get out on the upstream side you may get wetter, but it may be safer.

If the canoe does fill with water, it may be necessary to tear a hole in the downstream side of one end, so that the water pressure can be released and that end dragged round, upstream, to allow the canoe to slide off its obstruction.

Whatever happens, remember your capsize drill, and try to remain with your canoe. If by mischance you lose your paddle, your friends who are with you—for you should never paddle alone—can be despatched to gather it up. The only time when you should abandon your canoe is when you are being borne down upon some major danger, such as a weir or a waterfall. Then leave your canoe and swim as fast as you can to the side.

TAKE THE SHORTEST WAY

And talking of swimming to the side, swimmers are very slow. In clothes they are slower still. In clothes and towing a canoe they are even slower. It is imperative to get to the side as quickly as possible, even if it is only to be able to get into your canoe again and go on. Since you are so slow in the water, you must go by the shortest possible route. The shortest distance between a point (you) and a line (the bank) is at right angles to the line. Therefore swim directly towards the bank, even though you are being carried downstream by the current. You may end up some hundred yards down the river; but you will have got to the bank by the quickest possible route.

Just before or in rapids keep firm hold of one end of your canoe and follow it through the rapids. It will of its own accord find the deepest water and the safest passage, and will also protect you from the rocks.

EMPTYING YOUR CANOE

At the bank if your canoe is light, it may be possible for you to empty it by yourself without the assistance of your friends. Being at one end of your canoe, first establish a firm foothold. Now lift your end of the canoe as high as you can. When the water has finished pouring out, turn it over, up in the air; then lay it end down, and hold it there until all the water remaining in the canoe has run to your end. Then, putting one hand underneath, and the other on top, lift the canoe up and turn it over in one gesture. Continue to do this until all the water has come out of the canoe.

If the canoe is too heavy to do this, or there is too much water in it, two people are needed to empty it, one at each end. Throughout the initial operation the canoe must be kept on a dead even keel, fore and aft. Both people start lifting it slightly, and roll it over sideways until one edge of the cockpit coaming comes above the surface of the water. This breaks the airlock and the canoe will immediately start to rise. No one must hurry and the canoe must be kept level. As it comes up, the canoe will be rolled properly upside down again. When it is clear of the water, each person should lift his end in turn, until the canoe is again empty.

Some types of canoe have coamings specially contrived not to allow all the water out. The only thing to do with these canoes is to operate with two people, as above. Then, when all the water possible has been released by ordinary means, the canoe should be returned to a level, upside-down position above the water, and shaken by rolling from side to side until again all the water possible has been emptied out. After that there should be only a very little water left inside which, if you are fussy, you will have to mop up with a sponge.

Sometimes it is possible to lodge the far end of the canoe on the bank or on a rock. You then proceed as though with two people until the canoe is virtually empty. Then revert to the push-down/lift-up method, as with one person.

SMALL RAPIDS

The noise of falling water and the drop of the river in front of you will announce the rapid. You ought to know, from previous study of the map and the appropriate river guide, whether it is a severe one or not. If an easy one, the first man will go through some 30 yards ahead, thus allowing the second man time to avoid a collision and find a new route if the first man hits an obstruction. The rest of the party follow at similar intervals.

MORE SEVERE RAPIDS

Reconnaissance from the bank is essential. Careful note must be made beforehand of a nearby landmark so that the party can pull in to the bank in good time. Allow the most experienced canoeist to go through first, observed from the bank by the remainder. Only one canoeist should take the rapids at a time.

The whole party must wait in the first pool of quiet water until the last man is through and the party is complete again. No shame whatsoever is attached to portaging around a fall which is too severe for one's degree of experience.

At Sea

Much useful information about safety at sea is included in Norman Sudron's chapter on coastal touring. The repetition here of some of the main points will emphasize their importance.

1. Wear a BSI Kite-marked life-jacket (best of all the BCU approved life-jacket as advertised in this book and all canoeing magazines). So-called buoyancy aids are not adequate.

2. Pay particular attention to the state of your equipment. Salt water is harmful to all kinds of material, and sand inside a canvas canoe can wreak havoc between the ribs and the canoe skin. The efficiency of your buoyancy may be a life-saving matter.

3. Wear bright clothing. Orange is best, and excellent orange anoraks are available. Your canoe too should be a bright colour, easily visible at a long distance.

4. Three is the absolute minimum size of a party. Solo canoeing at sea is madness.

5. Take whistles and have a simple set of whistle and hand signals.

6. Consult knowledgeable local people—fishermen and harbour masters are best—about the local conditions.

7. Obtain the latest weather report from the nearest meteorological office.

8. Inform a reliable friend or a member of the family about your time and place of departure, your route, and your estimated time and place of arrival. Inform them when you land.

9. Adopt a definite formation at sea, with one nominated person in front and another to bring up the rear, no canoe being more than one minute's paddling time away from another, and all canoeists well positioned to keep an eye on one another all the time. The leader should be free to move around the party and keep in touch with everyone.

10. Experienced canoeists spurn the presence of a powered rescue boat, and their independence is for them one of the attractions of sea canoeing. But the less experienced should be under no illusions about the dangers of the sea. The rescue drills which follow must be known—and known well—by

K

everyone who ventures out; or the party must be accompanied by a power boat manned by a competent seaman with good local knowledge. Longer trips away from the coast should not be undertaken, even when accompanied by a rescue boat, without considerable training in overcoming the danger and discomfort of cramp and general fatigue when confined in a small canoe cockpit.

11. Learn and practise the Deep Water Rescue as often as possible. Capsizes tend to occur very quickly one after the other at sea, and the only sure preventative against panic is a high standard of training.

12. Do not hesitate to 'raft up' frequently to prevent fatigue setting in; but remember that a group of canoes rafted together will drift very quickly with current and tide.

13. In fact, never try to work against current and tide.

14. Learn the Eskimo Roll!

One of the joys of being advanced in anything is that one knows the rules of the game, and also when they must be broken. We mentioned earlier that in the capsize drill you must always leave your canoe upside down. In very heavy waves, however, as at sea, there is an argument for righting the canoe as quickly as possible; but we hope you will never find yourself in such conditions, until you too are an advanced canoeist.

In a heavy sea, if the canoe is left upside down, the airlock at the cockpit will be broken as the waves pass, and the canoe will fill up fairly quickly, and become waterlogged. The method of righting it under these conditions is then carried out like this.

Having blown his life-jacket up to maximum buoyancy, the canoeist goes to one side of his canoe, amidships, only holding it enough to prevent it from moving away. At that position he pushes his side upwards, with maximum thrust, trying as it were to chuck the canoe into the air. This will roll the canoe over to the right way up, with the minimum possible amount of water in it. This drill should be done as quickly as possible after the capsize, after which the canoeist returns once more to one end, where he holds on again, awaiting his friends' assistance.

The recognized method of putting someone back into his canoe again at sea is known as the

Deep Water Rescue Drill

This rescue is used when the 'patient' has done the capsize drill and is out of his canoe. At least two rescuers are needed.

The two canoes come up to the capsized one, to form a letter H. Both rescuers should face the same way, towards the on-coming waves. The patient should swim round to the outside of one of the rescuing canoes, and hold the cockpit coaming there. If there is another canoeist available, he should go to the outside of the other canoe and do likewise.

Both rescuers then proceed to lift the canoe, on a dead even keel, emptying it as for two people on the river's edge. As the casualty rises, it should be drawn across the decks of the two, to form a very stable catamaran. If there are only the two rescuers, then the one with the swimmer will start his lift slightly behind the other, so as to take a slightly greater load, since he cannot tip inwards because of the weight of the swimmer on his outside. It may be advisable for each rescuer to put his inward hand on top of the casualty, and do the lifting with his outward hand. This position of the hands is that of one of the rolls, and it will help him to right himself should he begin to capsize inwards.

Having emptied and righted the canoe, the two rescuers put it down between them, draw themselves together on it, and make a raft by holding their paddles across them. The swimmer then goes to the sterns, and comes between his own and one of the other canoes, just behind the cockpits. The remaining canoeist slides forward on the empty canoe and leans heavily on the forward deck. The swimmer then presses up on the after-decks of his two canoes and throws his feet into his own cockpit, immediately sliding into his seat, and is soon ready to set off again. With practice this rescue can be done under pretty severe conditions, excluding only actual breaking surf. Coolness and competence are more important than speed (except perhaps occasionally on a river, e.g. above a weir). Unlike the Eskimo Rescue, which follows, it can be done equally well with doubles as with singles.

THE ESKIMO RESCUE

When an Eskimo capsizes at sea and is unable to right his canoe again, perhaps because he has lost his paddle, he has very quickly to be rescued by a fellow hunter, yet without getting out of his canoe, for trying to swim in those icy waters would be fatal. We have adopted their technique of rescue. Incidentally, it helps greatly to build up your confidence

under water. It can only be done with a canoe which has a
tight-fitting spray cover, and which fits you tightly, with a
suitable knee-grip. It is no good if you fall out of the canoe as
soon as you turn upside down. Practise as follows: position
your own canoe at right angles to a friend's canoe. Grasp his
bow firmly. Lean over until your shoulder is in the water and
pull yourself upright. Lean over further each time until you are
eventually hanging completely upside down. Next, send your
friend a few feet away, turn upside down, and wait for him to
guide his bow into your hands. Send further and further away.
Now, when you capsize, bang the sides of your boat firmly to
attract his attention, then wave your hands back and forth on
either side and above your boat to make it easier for you to
find his bow. This is particularly important if the water is
dirty and you cannot see anything. As you gain confidence, you
will find that you can swim up on one side for a breath of air
whilst waiting for your rescuer. This is the best possible training
against panicking in an upturned canoe that we know.

A useful variation of the Eskimo Rescue is for the rescuer
to bring his boat parallel to the capsized canoe. The rescuer
places his paddle at right angles over his own cockpit and the
bottom of the upturned canoe. He guides the hands of the
canoeist under the water onto the shaft of the paddle between
the two boats. The canoeist in trouble then pulls himself up.
This variation is particularly valuable in rough water at sea:
there is much less danger of the rescuer's bows driving through
the side of the other canoe; and the canoeist who has been
rescued is at once in a very stable position, firmly linked as he
is with his rescuer's canoe.

THE ESKIMO ROLL
This is the technique which makes a canoeist really safe under
all conditions. It is now a requirement of the Advanced Sea
Proficiency Test. Don't try to learn it on your own, but join a
club where you can receive expert instruction. Many people
achieve their first roll after only twenty minutes' instruction,
although it takes many more hours' training and experience to
become really proficient.

There is no known guaranteed method for a single man to
get himself back into his canoe alone, after he has come out.
Therefore let us finish with a final law
NEVER CANOE ALONE.

9

Canoe Building

ALAN BYDE

CANOES may be built by many methods and there are books which will give step-by-step instructions on how to build a canoe. Unfortunately, no single book covers all methods of construction and they tend to reflect the enthusiasm of the author for particular building methods and fail to give straight-forward comparisons in terms of time, effort and skill needed. In this chapter I hope to do just this, and to guide you in your preliminary thinking before building a canoe.

Whatever constructional method you choose, it is important to realize that for the canoe to be safe it's design, construction, materials and safety features must be the best possible. The beginner's paddling faults may be corrected, but any faults in his canoe due to poor design or construction can seldom be rectified.

THE ESSENTIAL CANOE

In essence, the canoe is a method of fitting its occupant with a good underwater shape. This shape is provided in the design but its permanence is provided by the builder. The shape, or hull, of the canoe can be a hard skin made of laminations of resin and glass-fibres, or of wood veneers, or plywood, or planks of wood, or it may be a soft skin supported by stringers which in turn are supported by frames. Soft-skin canoes may be inflatable, and retain their shape by the air pressure within the several chambers in the construction.

The skin of the canoe may be load carrying, or simply a waterproof bag surrounding the load-carrying structure of the canoe. Whatever the structure considered, think of alternative ways in which you might obtain the desired result. It may be possible to have what is required with less expense, or more strength, or more adaptability, or more speed, or more stability, etc., in another method of construction.

What is it that you wish to know about the various methods of making a canoe? I would suggest that the following considerations should provide a useful answer.

Building Requirements
A. *Resources. Labour, tools, cash, time, skill.*
B. *Use of canoe.*
C. *Quality.*
D. *Quantity.*
E. *Maintenance and storage.*
F. *Kit/plans.*
G. *Type of skin.*
H. *Materials.*
I. *Fastenings.*
J. *Fittings.*
K. *Other advantages/disadvantages.*

Tools Required
This list includes all essential and many non-essential tools. What is essential for one type of canoe may not be so for another. What is essential for 'one-off' canoes may not be enough for production in numbers. I have numbered the tools for reference in the descriptions that follow, as repetitive lists are wasteful.

Reference		Description	Number
1	Saw	Panel	1
2		Coping	1
3		Keyhole	1
4		Jigsaw (Electric)	1
5		Set	1
6	Plane	Jack	1
7		Smoothing	1
8		Bullnose, rabbeting	1
9		Spokeshave, flat base	1
10		Spokeshave, curved base	1
11	Pliers	Sharp nose	1
12		Flat nose	1
13		Pincers	1
14	Hammer	Claw	1

15		Tack	1
16	Abrasives	File. Three-cornered saw sharpening	1
17		Rasp or 'Surform' tool	1
18		Sandpaper and block	quantity
19		Oil stone and oil	1
20		Disc sander (electric)	1
21	Screwdriver	Ratchet (not push type)	1
22		Ordinary	2
23	Clamps	3"	6
24		Mole grip wrench, 8" large	1
25	Drill	Hand, geared	1
26		Bits, $\frac{3}{8}$, $\frac{5}{16}$, $\frac{1}{4}$, $\frac{3}{16}$, $\frac{1}{8}$, $\frac{1}{16}$	1 each 2 each
27		Rosehead countersink bit	1
28	Brace	Carpenter's	1
29		Auger bits, 1", $\frac{1}{2}$", $\frac{3}{4}$"	1 each
30	Brushes	Good condition, 1" and 2"	1 each
31		Stubby condition 1" to 2"	4 or 5
32	Stapling gun	and alloy staples	1
33	Roller	Resin/glass laminates	1
34	Knife	'Stanley' trimming	1
35	Scissors	Large pair	1

Workshop Equipment

40	Bench	Carpenter's with vice	1
41	Trestles	6' × 2'	2
42	Block	Building 15' × 8$\frac{1}{2}$" × 2$\frac{1}{2}$" (approx)	1
43	Stool	Sawing	1
44	Tins	Empty 7 lb. jam	5 or 6
45	Jars	Glass, screw top	1 or 2

It is not essential to have all these tools, in fact, some canoe kits can be built with a saw, a screwdriver, and some sandpaper. If you are building only one, then buy a good kit at around £16 to £18. If you are building a number, as at a school, then most of the tools will probably be there to begin with. A stapling machine, or gun, is very useful for punching staples into thin ply, or veneers, or for attaching canvas to wooden frames. This stapling gun will cost about £5 for a good industrial type. An electric drill with jig saw and sanding attachments, and costing about £10 to £12, is a great effort-saver, but a coping saw costing a few shillings will do the same job in more time.

Generally, if you have good resources in equipment, time and effort will be saved. If you are very skilful with hand tools, mechanical aids may not be necessary, but then skill is usually a product of many years spent in working with hand tools, and this costs time and money in time past. An amateur builder can usually afford the time to make up for lack of skill, but great care must be taken not to compromise on quality in a small vessel which carries your life and the hopes and future of your nearest and dearest.

Building Methods Detailed

If you are about to build a canoe, the decision as to which one to choose must be yours, bearing in mind your own requirements. The needs of a canoeist on the upper Thames are not the same as those for a canoeist on the Clyde. The builder of one canoe for his own use will not require necessarily the same canoe as one to be used and built by schoolboys. In the brief descriptions of typical, and some untypical, canoes which follow, the reference letters and numbers given previously will be used in a tabulated commentary on the methods illustrated, which are:

Canvas, stringer, and frame. Rigid and folding.
Plywood, Kayel method, and ply on framework.
Glass/resin laminates. Cold moulding.
Wood veneer laminates. Cold moulding.

CANVAS, STRINGER AND FRAME

Sometimes known as a lath-and-canvas canoe, this craft consists of a number of frames cut from waterproof plywood, or built up from several pieces of small timber, to which are attached several stringers running fore and aft to give the canoe its shape. The framework is covered with canvas and then painted, or with PVC coated fabric which requires no painting.

A. *RESOURCES: Labour, Tools, Cash, Time, Skill*
It may be built by one person alone, or by several. More

than four can seldom be usefully employed on building one canoe. Tools and equipment, minimum, 1, 2, 14, 17, 18, 22, 24, 25, 26, 27, 30, 42, 43.

Cash. If you build a solo canoe from a kit, it will cost about £16 to £18. This will not include paddles and life-jacket or spray deck, and only rarely a good moulded plastic seat. Suitable canoe buoyancy will be another extra. You should have about £25 available to place a fully equipped canoe on the water. If the canoe is made from plans, these will cost including royalty, about 15s. and materials will have to be found locally. The cost will then range from about £7, if you have the resources of, say, a school or club workshop and bulk buying, to £12 for the bare canoe, plus extras as before.

Time. This will vary greatly according to ability. A skilled builder should use about thirty hours on an average canoe. A youngster working 'in the dark' on his own will find that he puts the frame together in a fine burst of enthusiasm, then slows down, and it may be a long time before the skin in put on (e.g. varnishing the woodwork is a tedious job and must be done well, with three coats if the frame is to last). Little obvious progress is shown at this stage. Perhaps double or treble the time for such a building project.

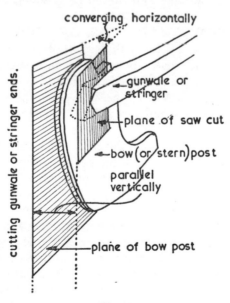

Fig. 27

Skill. This is fairly constant. Some kits have ready drilled holes, and cut mitres, but many kits require stringers to be cunningly angled and mitred in two planes, as at the bow and stern posts (Fig. 27). Cutting these mitres can be a frustrating job for a novice. Generally, most youngsters with average manual dexterity and aged about fourteen can tackle the job with some help. Most handymen could do the job successfully.

B. *USE OF CANOE* is best in deep waters where 'bump and scrape' conditions are not likely to be met. Launching conditions should be good, and care with the hull and deck is essential.

C. *QUALITY.* Such a canoe can be of very good quality, with excellent materials and workmanship, and some may be floating rubbish held together with paint and patches. Experience is the only safe guide when buying second-hand. Some quality may be reduced deliberately, as in the skin, but be ready to re-skin the job within two years if unproofed canvas is used.

D. *QUANTITY.* It is possible to design jigs in which these canoes may be built quickly and effectively. This is usually only worth while when it is proposed to build upwards of six canoes. Little time may be saved in building small numbers, and material cost is little altered by small numbers. One big advantage is in building skill developed, which will save time overall.

E. *MAINTENANCE AND STORAGE.* This type of canoe requires to be looked after with care. It should be washed out with fresh water after every occasion when it is used, especially on the sea, and on polluted rivers. This adds fifteen minutes to the canoeing session. Ask yourself, 'Do I mind spending time washing out canoes, when I could be spending time paddling them?'

Storage: this should be in a covered well-ventilated place off the ground, to allow air to circulate all round. It should be stored upside down to permit drainage. The supports should not rub the deck and hull canvas.

F. *KITS AND PLANS.* I would advise beginners to buy a good kit. Kit qualities vary, and designs vary, so please, please, ensure that the advice of a knowledgeable person is first obtained. Some types of canoe are suitable only for certain waters. Until you have some experience, as after building or helping to build a kit, it is preferable to build a kit rather than work from plans. Materials are sometimes not easy to find, and can be expensive, and often no real saving is achieved in terms of cost per hours of satisfactory use.

G. *TYPE OF SKIN.* This is, of course, a soft-skin canoe.

H. *MATERIALS.* Frames should be about half-inch marine plywood (Fig. 28). Water and boil proof (WBP) ply will do, but may not last as well as good marine ply. Phenol bonded ply, WBP, is acceptable. Phenol bonded birch plys are tough to cut, and I have not seen marine quality birch ply. Thinner ply may be used for extra reinforcement around the cockpit where most of the stresses on the canoe are concentrated. Three millimetre is the thinnest usually acceptable, 4 mm. is better, but more expensive, and one-third as heavy again. 1½ mm. birch ply is obtainable.

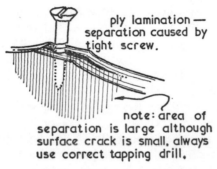

ply lamination — separation caused by tight screw.

note: area of separation is large although surface crack is small, always use correct tapping drill.

Fig. 28

Stringers are the strength, and the resilience of the hull. They *must* be knot free. Minor knots may be accepted but those that interfere with more than ten per cent of the section of the stringer are useless (Fig. 29). Bend the stringer firmly. (How much bend is that?) If the stringer breaks at the knot, then it wasn't any use anyway. Mahogany type woods for stringers are beautiful to look at, difficult to build with because of their contrary grain, heavy when built in, and fracture easily on impact. Canary pine is often recommended, because of its straight grain and smooth appearance. It is not heavy, but it is brittle, and snaps fairly readily when twisted, as must usually be done at bow and stern posts. It also shatters on impact. By far the best wood is aircraft quality spruce, but it is about three times the cost of mahogany, if you can get it. Sitka spruce is very good, but rare, and costly. For all-round good service, I prefer ordinary redwood, carefully selected. The timber-yard

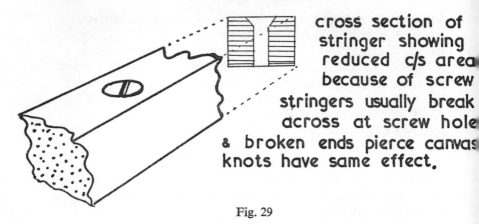

cross section of stringer showing reduced c/s area because of screw stringers usually break across at screw hole & broken ends pierce canvas knots have same effect.

Fig. 29

foreman will know where he can lay hands on a special bit of timber, and he will then have to render it into small sections, shove the lot through the planer, reject knotty bits, and then have a youngster look at him soulfully, and ask how much it is. If the boy gets his wood under £3, the foreman is of the stuff saints are made.

Canvas skins. Anything that will form a watertight covering will not do. Cheese cloth soaked in resin has been used, old railway tarpaulins also. Generally, it has been found that the cost of a good skin is little compared with the dangers into which one may be thrown by poor materials. The minimum acceptable is 12 oz. vat-dyed canvas. Green rot-proof canvas, 18 oz., is very serviceable, and fairly easy to put on. PVC impregnated canvas materials, sold under such names as 'Tufskin' and 'Tynehide' are good. Super grades are available at greater cost. A material used for lorry covers, PVC impregnated Terylene sheet, is good for racing canoes where toughness and light weight are more important than raised cost, but it has a curious lack of resistance to abrasive rubbing over the stringers. Rubberized multi-ply cotton skins are available, being very good value and fairly costly, but now giving place to plastic impregnated materials. Pure sheet plastic is dangerous in use, as in cold weather it will fracture, and without fibrous reinforcement will split irremediably and extensively. Sticking plasticized sheets together is rarely a satisfactory job. As few, if any, solvents seem to mingle with the plastic surface to produce a good union this makes repairs difficult on wet hulls.

NOTE: Damage to canvas skins is almost always directly

under where a frame crosses the canvas, or along the edge of a stringer, which has a guillotine effect. What happens is that an obstruction presses the canvas inwards, and if this depression is big enough the canvas will be cut on its own framework.

I. *FASTENINGS*. Screws used are often brass. A word of warning, brass is an alloy of copper and zinc. Electrolytic action especially in sea water will leach out the zinc in the alloy, and the screw becomes a tiny 'honeycomb' of copper, friable and weak. (The copper salts then stain the wood around the hole.) This process is called 'de-zincification'. Use gunmetal screws. The most useful size is 1-inch, or 1¼-inch No. 6, countersunk, *gunmetal*. Slotted head screws are supplied unless Phillips' headed screws are required.

J. *METAL FITTINGS*. Brass suspect as before. Aluminium is obtainable in many alloys, and some are resistant to electrolytic action and some are not. Magnesium alloys literally vanish in sea water. Pure aluminium puts on a skin of oxide very rapidly, and resists corrosion after that, but is so soft as to be of little constructional use, except perhaps as rubbing strips on the outside of the hull.

Fittings for the hull include rudders, seats, knee braces, back rests, foot bars and rudder bars, and wires, lockers, etc. I will select a few. Rudders are usually best bought from canoe manufacturers who supply them at about £3 each with all wires and fittings. If you have the right materials and know what you are doing (it is then unlikely that you will need this advice), then you will make your own. A great deal of satisfaction may be had from making a useful thing like a rudder, making it well, and then using it. (Suggested for metal work for boys in their last year at school.) Rudders are needed at sea, for racing, and sailing but hardly ever for any other purpose.

Back-rests. The purist will not have a back-rest, as the seasoned canoeist naturally leans slightly forward. Back-rests are available which consist of a slightly curved piece of ply which is fixed to a slightly hollowed and rounded bar, which in turn pivots on two screws, let one into either end of the end grain of the bar. These screws pivot in brass brackets which stick out at right angles to the back part of the coaming frame. In time the bar and rest are lost, and the brackets dig holes in the back. The unpadded ply will also rub against the back, and the spinous processes start to rub through the skin from the inside out, against the friction and pressure applied by the

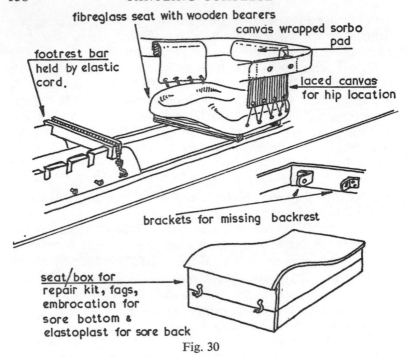

fibreglass seat with wooden bearers

canvas wrapped sorbo pad

footrest bar held by elastic cord.

laced canvas for hip location

brackets for missing backrest

seat/box for repair kit, fags, embrocation for sore bottom & elastoplast for sore back

Fig. 30

unpadded ply 'back-rest'. If a back-rest is to be used, wrap sorbo rubber in waterproof canvas, and attach that directly to the coaming frame at the back, without complicated brackets.

Seat. Please treat the neatly shaped box, which holds all your bits and pieces, with grave suspicion. It takes time to make and is rarely comfortable except for people whose bottoms are curved in one plane only. Flat pieces of ply are torture after an hour if unpadded, and if padded, the pad may be lost, or soak up wet, or come loose, and you will slip about in the cockpit. My best advice is to remember that you may be a long way from shore, and unable to move about and ease the aching backside, and restore sensation to the numbly aching legs. Go for comfort. A good and simple resin/glass laminate seat will cost about 18s., is shaped in three dimensions, and is made with the contours of the human behind in mind (Fig. 30).

I have dealt in detail with seats, and back-rests, but this is where you make contact with the canoe, and this is where you will suffer if things are not right.

K. *OTHER ADVANTAGES AND DISADVANTAGES.* This type of canoe is well known, and detailed advice on how to build one is readily available. Construction uses conventional skills, and materials are not hard to come by (with reservations). They require constant care, and if they rip they leak very rapidly, as the canvas bags inwards under water pressure. The skin is easily repaired by patching with hull material, large rips should be sewn first. They do not take an efficient underwater shape, compared with a good hard skin canoe. Their life is about three years of hard use, before a new skin and substantial frame repairs are required. For all their need for constant care, they do give good service if well built. Time required to make them compares well with any other kind of canoe. When carrying gear in them the frames are an obstruction, but they make handy anchorage points.

FOLDING CANOES

The folding canoe is basically the same method of construction as the lath-and-canvas canoe, but the framework is so constructed that it can be taken to pieces for ease of transport.

These can be built by the amateur, but take so much time and skill that they are not a proposition for anyone but the enthusiast who has considerable wood and metal working skill, and who can shape, stitch, and fit (without wrinkles) the expensive rubberized fabric skin. Metal fittings must be made to fit and keep on fitting, and the best wood is straight grained ash, which is expensive and not easy to obtain. I have not built a folding canoe but I have talked with someone who has and he did not recommend it. They do have the advantage of fitting into bags for carrying, but they usually weigh about 40 to 50 lb. and this takes a bit of humping in awkward-shaped bags. A wet skin is very difficult to refit after it has been removed, and a skin which has dried off the canoe requires much brute force to refit. A ready-made canoe will cost about £50; home-made about £25. It is possible to have the skin professionally made, and if you are determined to build a folding canoe this is worth considering.

PLYWOOD, KAYEL METHOD, AND PLY ON FRAME

The Kayel method of construction, developed by K. H. Littledyke, for chine canoes consists of cutting the sides and bottom from plywood and then joining these panels at 2-inch intervals with soft copper wire. The joints are then sealed with glass-fibre tape, resulting in a light but strong hull.

A. *RESOURCES*

The Kayel method lends itself to supervised mass building. Schoolchildren in numbers may be occupied in twisting the wire ties together, although physical limitations restrict the maximum working number on one canoe to six. It can be built by one person quite well. Tools, minimum requirements, 1, 2, 9, 12, 14, 17, 18, 22, 25, 26, 27, 30, 45.

Cash: kits are available at about £13 to £17. The resin and glass kits supplied are usually sufficient, but some of the kits for larger canoes require more resin, etc. This is a very costly way to buy resin, catalyst, and accelerator, but for one-off jobs it is the only practical way. For numbers, you can buy in bulk with considerable saving. If you buy a kit, all the necessary materials are provided, and some have the cockpit rims, or coamings, ready laminated. Kits are available in various degrees of completeness, and they contain detailed instructions for building. These canoes can be built from plans, which cost about 15s. and the material cost is about £7 to £10 for the bare hull for the smaller designs.

Time. This canoe will take about thirty hours, the progress is continuous, and less tedious for the youngster. *Skill.* This is not of the same order as that needed for a canvas canoe. The shaping of the ply panels can be done by youngsters under supervision, but there comes a stage when the panels are being assembled, when the experienced eye will detect a bumpy looking line and change it into a smooth shape (Fig. 31). Again, mixing the resin properly can be done by children under supervision, but the sense of urgency with which one must

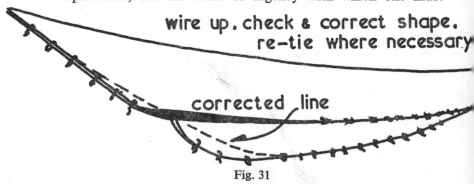

wire up. check & correct shape.
re-tie where necessary

corrected line

Fig. 31

13. Easy, relaxed control of the canoe in fast water, achieved by good weight distribution and use of the paddle

14. A pair from East Germany tackle the final gates of a slalom course in a Canadian canoe. Note the rescue man at the ready (top right)

15. An early morning paddle on the River Arno, in Florence. In the
background the famous Ponte Vecchio

16. K2s battling for the lead

handle mixed synthetic resins may be lacking in unsupervised youngsters. A logical mind is useful in working on this type of canoe, where organization of workers pays dividends.

B. *USE OF CANOE.* This type of canoe fulfils much the same requirements as the canvas skin canoe, there being equivalent models of each type. It is useful in deep waters and the sea, being strong. Great care need not be taken, and bump and scrape rivers will not cause so much immediate difficulty, but maintenance will usually be a workshop job. Roughly half-yearly visits to the workshop have been necessary with an Eskimo kayak I built, for replacement of the external resin/glass seams on the canoe which have been damaged and which tend to separate from the ply unnoticed, allowing water to seep into the hull via the joints (Fig. 32). These seepage faults are hard to find, and can usually only be cured by the complete retaping of joints. The canoe in question is in constant use in swimming baths in the winter, and on the sea and river in the summer. Chlorinated bath water seems to shorten the life of the resin, but not seriously.

C. *QUALITY.* This is set by the plywood used. This *must* be marine ply. Three-millimetre material is good, and light, and robust enough. Four-millimetre ply will last longer, weigh a third as much again, and cost more. The heavier ply is good for a school canoe which is subject to rough usage.

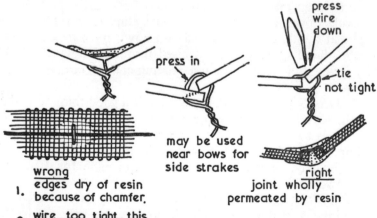

press
wire
down

press in

tie
not tight

press in

may be used
near bows for
side strakes

wrong
edges dry of resin
because of chamfer.

right
joint wholly
permeated by resin

1. edges dry of resin because of chamfer.
2. wire too tight. this lifts tape, causing bubble.
3. any part of joint where there is no resin water will penetrate.

Fig. 32

L

D. *QUANTITY*. If built in numbers, it is good for bulk buying of resin and glass tape. Plans would then be the better proposition. A kit is good to begin with. Inform the supplier of kits if you intend to build more than one canoe from one set of plans, as royalties are due to the designer. If a number are built in a school, children become accustomed to working on them, and turn out quite good jobs.

E. *MAINTENANCE AND STORAGE*. They can be left outside, off the ground. Careful storage will lengthen their lives, but the consequences of neglect are not so disastrous as for a canvas canoe.

F. *KIT/PLANS*. Kits are good; plans are better when you have knowledge of the method used (which it is unlikely that you will have without building one of these). After the first kit, use plans. Kits save time looking for materials. Plans save cash.

G. *TYPE OF SKIN*. It is a hard-skin canoe. I prefer it to soft-skin canoes, for most purposes.

H. *MATERIALS*. Already dealt with.

I. *FASTENINGS*. These are copper wire ties. I find that bits of cable that the electrician cuts off when working are excellent. 7/·004 twin with earth, that is about 40 amp. cable, or 3/·036 twin with single ·044 earth do very well. 7/·029 is a bit too fine. This wire, when the insulation has been burnt or stripped off and cut into 4-inch lengths, makes excellent ties. Fewer screws are used than in a canvas canoe, and brass drive pins fasten the decks down. I have lately bought a stapler, and it bangs in staples at twenty times the speed of a boy using a tack hammer with his hand sprouting five bruised thumbs. Staples fix decks very well. Steel staples are not recommended because of corrosion.

J. *FITTINGS*. As before. A spray deck is a good thing to make, and the Kayel canoes have cockpits (Figs. 33 & 34) which lend themselves to the fitting of spray decks with elasticated edges, an important safety point. Spray decks may be bought for £2 approximately, or made on a sewing machine for 10s. and about two hours work.

K. *OTHER ADVANTAGES*. When the ply is shattered by heavy impact, it does not bulge in underwater pressure to the same extent that canvas does, and one may canoe with a slowly leaking hull for quite a long way. Repair is a workshop job and is not so difficult as it would be to strip off canvas to get at a shattered stringer away from the cockpit opening. The main

spray deck for oval cockpit

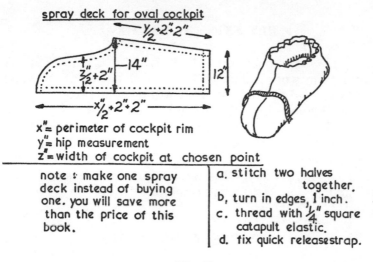

$x'' =$ perimeter of cockpit rim
$y'' =$ hip measurement
$z'' =$ width of cockpit at chosen point

note : make one spray deck instead of buying one. you will save more than the price of this book.	a. stitch two halves together. b, turn in edges, 1 inch. c. thread with $\frac{1}{4}''$ square catapult elastic. d. fix quick release strap.

Fig. 33

oval cockpit

scrap ply pieces overlapping form rim

sorbo knee pads

6 mm.
12 mm.
6 mm.
section of rim.

rim, lip for spray deck.

shape this edge before fixing.

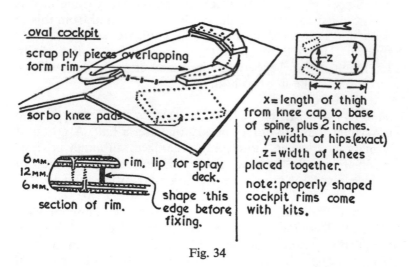

$x =$ length of thigh from knee cap to base of spine, plus 2 inches.
$y =$ width of hips.(exact)
$. z =$ width of knees placed together.

note: properly shaped cockpit rims come with kits.

Fig. 34

disadvantage that I have found is the susceptibility to seepage, and the regular visits to the workshop to be dried off (resin will not cure properly in the presence of moisture) and retaped along a seam. It is possible to make a very pretty looking boat with a painted hull leaving the deck well-varnished marine ply. On the whole I prefer it to the canvas canoe.

PLY SKIN ON FRAME

This is the traditional method of building a chine hull. A skeleton framework is built and is then planked with plywood which is secured to the framework with glue and pins.

Some older designs still use this method. It results in a canoe looking like the Kayel type, and almost any single chine canvas canoe may be skinned in ply instead. This makes a stronger canoe, a much heavier one, it costs more than the canvas or Kayel but it does not require knowledge of resin glass laminations. Not for my recommendation.

GLASS RESIN LAMINATES

Glass-fibre canoes are produced by laying either glass matting or cloth inside a mould and then applying polyester resin as a filler. Since only the surface next to the mould is smooth, it is necessary first to make a male mould in wood, and from this to take a female mould in glass resin laminate which, suitably supported, is used for producing the finished canoe shells. The mould must be perfect since any irregularities will be transferred to the finished hull.

A. *RESOURCES, etc.*

Labour. A hull can be built by no less than two people, who know what they are doing, in an hour and a half. A group of six schoolboys when thoroughly organized, although novices, can do the job in the same time. It is an excellent method of building several canoes. It is not a sound proposition for the 'one-off' job. *Tools.* 1, 2, 14, 17, 18, 22, 25, 26, 27, 30, 31, 33, 44. *Cash.* Averages out about £7 for the resin/glass laminate shell only, plus deck and cockpit fittings about £4 extra. If novices do the job, wastage will account on average for another £3 per canoe. *Time.* About two hours to lay up the hull, plus about twenty hours to fit the decks, etc. I should be honest and state that the two hours' lay-up is for from two to six people, a gross time of from four to twelve hours. *Skill.* This is mostly in organization. The physical skill consists of dabbing motions with the short brushes, stippling resin into the glass-fibres, and knowing where to put the strips and sheets of glass fibre. The organization is all important.

1. Clear the workshop of dust and rubbish, have the area around the job clear for easy movement.

2. Prepare a table top that is clean and about 6 by 2 ft. This is for cutting up the glass-fibre mat and cloth.

3. Appoint resin mixer, glass cutter(s), glass layer, and resin handlers (brush) and a roller. You must supervise. DO NOT join in.

4. It is vitally important that the resin handlers should not handle uncut glass and that the glass layer should stand clear of the glass cutter and not stick him up. The glass cutter must keep his hands absolutely clean of resin.

5. Everyone MUST use barrier cream. The Inspector of Factories, Ministry of Labour, has published a workshop chart illustrating the dangers of dermatitis through frequent use of resinous chemicals.

I give detail here so that the difference between the skill of a good woodworker, and that of the good resin/glass laminate builder may be illustrated. Details of how to build in this material may be had from the magazine *Canoeing*, issues from December 1963 to March 1964 inclusive, or from Bill Saunders, CCPR, 40 Saddler Street, Durham City, or from *Complete Amateur Boat Building*, Michael Verney, published by John Murray, 1961, at £1. This is very good, but does not deal specifically with canoes.

B. *USE OF CANOE*. Almost anywhere, strong and 'bash' resistant.

C. *QUALITY*. Usually good, but suffers from 'blooming' of the resin through presence of damp, and thin laminations can result in porosity. This is usually the result of insufficient rolling or stippling, to get the air out of the glass and resin. When well made, better than most other methods.

D. *QUANTITY*. Casting from the mould is easy. Lining up as with frames and stringers is not necessary, as the mould passes on faithfully all its good and bad points to every shell moulded.

E. *MAINTENANCE AND STORAGE*. The least troublesome of any. It may be left on the ground without serious damage for months in winter, and still be ready for immediate use after a rub over.

F. *KIT/PLANS*. This is not a job for plans. Kits are obtainable, and very good they are, which provide ready moulded hulls with inwales already built in so that the decks can be fitted by the home builder. These kits cost about £20, and are well worth it. The types available are specialized. Line drawings are available from the magazine *Canoeing* which will give the designers' shapes, and leave the building of the model and then the mould to the ingenuity of the builder.

G. *TYPE OF SKIN.* A hard-skin canoe, with similar reaction to impact as the ply canoe, but more resistant to impact. Repairs present workshop problems, and must be carried out in a damp-free atmosphere.

H. *MATERIALS.* There are now many suppliers of resins and glass. You will not usually get these materials in sufficient quantity from a handyman shop. They must be ordered from the manufacturer in quantity, such as a thirty pound drum of resin, enough for three canoes, at 3s. 6d. per pound; catalyst, which is expensive, and accelerator will also be required.

I. *FASTENINGS.* These must be attached to the hull by resin. Holding the attachments whilst the setting, or curing, of the resin takes place, requires some form of clamp. These can be improvised, but the purchase of 3-inch G clamps saves a great deal of fiddling about.

J. *FITTINGS.* It is bad practice to mould parts onto the bottom, or near to the bottom of the hull, as the hull derives a lot of its advantages from resilience under impact, and stiffening it by putting in fittings, such as a seat fixed to the floor, localizes impact stresses and damage is more likely. In any case, the fitting tends to separate quite soon. Seats, etc., are best suspended from the cockpit opening, or from high up the sides of the hull, near the inwale.

K. *ADVANTAGES AND DISADVANTAGES.* Advantages are very clear for the school wishing to build a number of canoes both because of ease of maintenance, and the useful point of team work for efficient working. The glass-fibre canoe is tough, and will probably give 30 per cent longer life than a ply or canvas canoe, say five as against three to four years. Disadvantages are that it requires numbers of people to build, although I do know one man who turned out a number of these, on his own, taking from 6.30 p.m. to 11.30 p.m. each evening for each shell. It is subject to porosity unless very well built, and avoiding this comes with experience. It is slightly heavier than canvas or ply, 40 lb. as against 30 to 35 lb. It requires real organizing ability, and this is usually obtained only by attending a course and doing it, or setting out 'in the dark', and making mistakes. Written work now available should reduce errors.

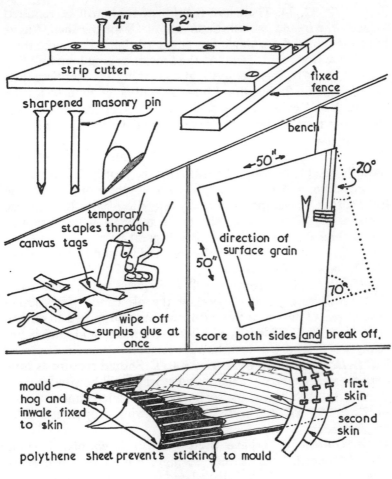

Fig. 35

WOOD VENEER LAMINATES

Cold-moulded wood veneer canoes usually consist of three
skins of veneer strips laid diagonally at right angles to each
other. Briefly, the construction method consists of laying the
strips over a male mould, holding them temporarily in position
with staples, and then glueing the next layer in position
(Fig. 35).

A. *RESOURCES, etc.*

For one to six people. *Tools,* for the shell only, 2, 17, 22, 25,

26, 27, 30, 32, 34. The usual full kit of tools will be required to build the mould as well. *Cash*, about £8 for the shell. I have built the mould for a single for under £4, but I know the foreman at the woodyard. *Time*. At the time of writing I am building my first canoe by this method and it is taking a longer time than usual, and I am finding that I have used difficult material for the design. I will guess, and say about thirty hours, maybe less when production methods have been developed. *Skill*. For building the mould, the usual woodworking skill, but the casting consists of laying up 2-inch strips of $1\frac{1}{2}$ mm. ply, held temporarily in place with staples. This is largely a matter of organization, and can be taught to a novice group when one has thoroughly grasped the ideas oneself. Ability to visualize what happens to curving sheets of material when wrapped round three dimensional moulds is a great help.

B. *USE*, probably as for the resin/glass laminated canoe. Should be good for schools.

C. *QUALITY*. This promises well. I will guess again, and suggest that it will be equally as good as the ply canoe, with design advantages of curves in three dimensions as opposed to chines.

D. *QUANTITY*. This is for building from a mould, and is not really worth while for less than six canoes.

E. *MAINTENANCE AND STORAGE*. Should require as little maintenance as the ply canoe, and storage will be similar.

F. *KIT/PLANS*. As for the resin/glass laminated canoe.

G. *TYPE OF SKIN*. Hard-skin, with flexing properties similar to glass/resin.

H. *MATERIALS*. I have used Finnish birch ply, $1\frac{1}{2}$ mm. phenol bonded. This is very springy, but in two-inch strips it is manageable. I have had to bend it over curves of less than two-inch radius, and this is almost impossible. Veneers will respond much more readily to bending than that, although they will be less strong. Bending ply strips is improved by cutting the material at an angle across the face of the ply, so that the grain runs slanting across the length of the ply strips at about 60 to 70 degrees to the short edge. Glue must be stable after setting, and I have used Aerolite 306, which uses a formic acid hardener. Small kits of glue can be bought for 6s. or so. This is financial suicide on a job of this size. Buy a 7 lb. drum of resin powder for less than £1, and the acid in 16 oz. bottles is not expensive. The staples must be noncorrosive, alloy will do.

I. *FASTENINGS.* On this job I have used 3,500 staples at 16s. per 5,000. I should economize when I know the job better. Screws, about three dozen 1 inch No. 6.

J. *FITTINGS.* As for resin glass laminates.

K. *ADVANTAGES.* Much the same as for resin/glass laminates, and once started it may be left temporarily unfinished, unlike resin/glass which must be finished at one go. In use it should prove as resilient as resin/glass. *Disadvantages.* One, it is as rare as resin/glass methods, and few people may be found to advise who have actually done the job. It is a fiddly job getting the ply strips to lie down, and to avoid bubbles under the laminations, but this should be avoided with practice.

TOWARDS THE FUTURE

With the tremendous development in plastics and synthetics it is possible that within a few years none of the methods described in this chapter will be in common use. The canoe builder with an inventive turn of mind will constantly be looking for new ideas and new materials from which he can create his dream boat. I, myself, have several notions I hope to try out before long. However, to all would-be experimenters I would stress the point I made at the beginning of this chapter: a canoe must be suited to the purpose of its paddler and unless this rule is followed you may finish up with something beautiful but useless.

10

Fun and Games in Your Canoe

BRIAN SKILLING

IT may seem strange that a book largely devoted to the challenging aspects of canoeing should include a chapter whose main theme is 'messing about'. It has been included, however, for two reasons; first, that many canoeists, particularly in schools and youth clubs, have to spend a large part of the time on one stretch of water and may be in danger of becoming bored by its familiarity, and second, the belief of the author that indulging in stunts and games in a canoe can lead to a greater understanding of the capabilities of both the canoeist and his craft. With this in mind, the following are some ideas on which the imaginative may base a rag regatta, which as a money-raising spectator event is likely to be more successful than a straight regatta, or which may be used as a way of relaxation after a tough training session, or which can be practised simply for fun.

THE WIGGLE AND WRIGGLE TESTS

These two tests were originally designed by the slalom canoeists to enable them to develop their boat control on still water, and to retain a measure of progress by paddling against the clock. The equipment needed is simple and can be erected on any slow moving stretch of water or in a swimming pool. A number of clubs run the 'Wiggle and Wriggle test' on a seasonal basis using a 'ladder' chart to show progress and awarding a prize at the end of the season for the paddler at the top of the ladder, and a second prize for the canoeist who has climbed the most steps of the ladder during the season.

The 'Wiggle and Wriggle' tests were first published in a magazine called *White Water*, and the following is an extract of the original article:

We have designed a standard series of manœuvres to be carried out on a standard slalom gate on standard water conditions. For the first time, therefore, we are able to compare the performance of a canoeist in Perth, Scotland with that in Perth, Australia. Not only that, we can compare the ability of a canoeist today and in ten years' time. This we feel is by far the most important thing. It enables any would-be slalomist to check how his boat handling is effected by his training techniques. It can be used to compare boats, paddles and so on. It can, alas, tell you when you are passing your peak.

It also, we hope, will give some stimulus to gate practice, for, from our own experience, we know that there is an ample enthusiasm for rough water work, but gate practice is usually thought of as a necessary evil of slalom. After great deliberation we have kept the tests as simple as possible.

We have stuck to a single gate, wide enough to cope with canadian canoes as well as folding and rigid kayaks. The test must be 'clean', that is, no poles should be touched at all. Beginners may find it useful, however, to be allowed to add penalties according to the slalom rules. This will give them a measure of progress. The first test, the 'Wiggle', can be carried out by any canoeist. The second, advanced, test is called the 'Wriggle', the extra 'r' denoting rolling. This is for the advanced slalomist, and calls for four eskimo rolls, just prior to passing through the gate at specified points. This not only means fast rolling, but also fast appreciation of the position when the roll is complete.

The test must be carried out PRECISELY as laid down.

The Gate Itself

This consists of two poles suspended by line from two screw eyes in a horizontal spacer bar. The screw eyes should be 48 inches plus the thickness of the pole apart, thus making the space between the poles exactly 48 inches. The poles should be attached to the lines in such a manner that the poles can hang vertically. The poles should be hung so that their lower ends are two inches above the water. The tests must be carried out on still water.

The Test

The run must be clean. That is, the poles must not be touched by canoe, paddle, or body. The canoeist should take up position about a boat's length from the gate. Timing starts as the bow enters the gate for the first time, and ends 'nine gates later' as the bow leaves the gate—the ninth gate being a reverse gate. The sequence MUST be adhered to, and is as follows:

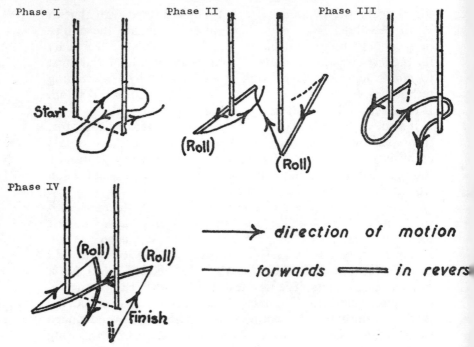

Fig. 36

Forward, Gate 1, then turn to starboard and come back through for forward, Gate 2, then turn to port and go through for forward, Gate 3. This is shown diagrammatically as 'Phase 1' (Fig. 36). You now reverse past and to the right of the gate, then do forward, Gate 4. Now reverse past and to the left of the gate, then do forward, Gate 5. This is represented in 'Phase II'. The rest of the gates are now reverse gates. Once again reverse past and to the left of the gate, then turning anti-clockwise, do reverse Gate 6R, then turning clockwise, do Gate reverse 7R. This completes 'Phase III'. The final phase, 'Phase IV' completes the test as follows. Go forward past, and to the right of the gate, then do reverse Gate 8R. When clear of the gate, go forward past and to the left of the gate, then do reverse Gate 9R. The test ends as the bow clears the gate.

The Wriggle

This is as for the Wiggle except that four rolls have been introduced. The direction and technique of rolling is not specified, but the rolls must be through 360 degrees, i.e. down one side, up the other. All rolls must take place just before tackling a gate, certainly no sooner than the 'points' shown in the diagrammatic 'course'.

CANOE POLO

Since the earliest days of sporting canoeing there are records of some form of canoe polo being played. The rules, however, have never been standardized and it is never considered anything but a bit of light-hearted sport. The main consideration when organizing a game of canoe polo is to ensure that the canoes are not damaged, and this can happen very easily if the referee does not keep a firm hand on the game.

The following rules are those used by Oliver Cock, BCU National Coach, and are based on his experience in running training courses in many parts of the country. They would seem to reduce the likelihood of damage to canoes to the minimum whilst retaining the maximum element of excitement.

Rules

1. An area of reasonably still water, about the size of a football pitch is required. A very slow-flowing river will do. If the river is wide, play across it. If the stretch of water is narrow, like a canal, play along it, Mark off the goals at each end by bushes, posts, or any other means. The full width of the pitch is the goal.

2. Play with a plastic football.

3. Approximately five players to each side, although four or six will do. Three is too few and seven-a-side is beginning to be a crowd.

4. Play approximately seven minutes each way. No half-time interval.

5. The ball should be picked up and thrown or punched. The paddle must *not* be used to play the ball, except to stop it in flight.

Clubs organizing canoe polo for the first time often permit the ball to be hit with the paddle, but this can be dangerous and it is all too easy for somebody's head to be accidentally swiped instead of the ball.

6. Play in single-seater kayaks. Doubles are just not manoeuvrable enough.

7. If there is a collision, both parties are disqualified. This is a safety rule because in a collision one canoe goes through the other and may even injure the occupant of the canoe receiving the blow. Disqualified paddlers may be allowed to play again after half time. The referee must interpret this rule with common sense; side brushes are quite acceptable and should not lead to disqualification.

8. Whatever a player gets hold of, he must get rid of it at once. Therefore, if a player gets the ball he must throw it at once. There is no penalty for disobeying this rule other than the bad language of the enemy. If a player insists in putting the ball inside his canoe then the referee should point out that it is spoiling the game. If a player can seize an adversary's paddle, he is entitled to do so but he must, obviously, throw it away at once.

9. If a player can seize one of the opposition, *whether he has the ball or not*, he can get rid of him by capsizing him, but he is not allowed to hold him upside down.

THE SPIRIT OF THE GAME IS TO GET RID OF THE ENEMY. THEN YOU CAN SCORE AS MANY GOALS AS YOU LIKE.

HAND PADDLING RACE

As its name implies, in this race paddlers leave their paddles behind and propel themselves by means of their hands. This is best achieved by dipping both hands in the water at the same time, leaning well forward to make the longest possible stroke. Alternatives are to equip each paddler with two plates, mugs, table tennis bats, or some similar objects. Do not make the course too long as progress is rather slow. Hand paddling races can also be held with the canoes being propelled backwards which gives greater speed but requires more skill in steering.

A variation is to scatter the water about fifty yards away from the paddlers with the appropriate number of touring paddles (one for each boat) split into their two parts. Competitors must then hand paddle up to the floating paddles, find a matching pair and then return by conventional paddling to the starting point. First home is the winner.

BROOM RACE

Each paddler is given two brooms and a length of cord or rope.

The object is to lash the two brooms together so that there is a bristled head at each end and then, using this as substitute paddle, the canoeist can propel himself over the designated course.

Alternatives are to give each competitor just one broom and let them paddle their kayaks using the broom as a single blade paddle. Or, to give the competitors their brooms already lashed and treat the event as a straightforward race.

BACKWARDS RACE

Start with the sterns pointing along the course and have a simple straightline race with the canoeists paddling backwards. If there is enough room, race over a triangular course, thus requiring the paddlers to turn the canoes—but in this case make certain that the first turn is sufficiently far away to enable the competitors to string out, otherwise too much bunching on the turns may result in damage to the canoes. A variation is to require the competitors to paddle the first half of a straight course paddling conventionally, and then to paddle backwards to the starting line, which is now the finish.

SITTING ON THE STERN RACE

Paddlers sit astride the stern decks of their canoes with their feet in the water. In this position the bows will be high out of the water and the course of the canoes likely to be erratic. See that all paddlers are equally far back on the decks of their canoes and thus under the same handicap, moving forward during the race disqualifies. The race should be over a fairly short course.

STANDING RACE

Competitors propel their canoes from a standing position with feet inside the cockpit. Check that all paddles are about the same length, check also that the construction of competing canoes is suitable for this event particularly if soft-skinned boats are being used.

SINGLE-BLADED KAYAK RACE

Standard double-bladed paddles are used for this event, but

competitors may only paddle on one side of the canoe, i.e. they must propel their boats using Canadian canoe techniques. The choice of paddling side may be left to each competitor. If the paddlers are reasonably competent at propelling their canoes in this fashion, a more challenging variation is to require them to cover half the course paddling only on the left hand side of their canoes, turn round a buoy, and then come back to the starting point paddling on the right-hand side of their canoes. It will be found that few kayakers can paddle with equal facility on both sides of their canoe using a single-bladed paddle stroke.

SIDEWAYS RACE

Competitors propel their canoes sideways using either a draw-stroke or a sculling stroke. The course should be a short one such as across a river or swimming bath. This event is a suitable one for a 'there and back' course which demands the use of the paddle on both sides of the canoe.

SUBMARINE RACE

Use kayaks of the slalom type with small cockpits, kneegrips, and spray covers. Competitors line up with their canoes at right angles to the course. At the starting command, they must capsize, and then *whilst remaining in the canoes* swim to the surface and using their arms swim their canoes to the finish. A very short course only is used in this event which is well suited to form part of a rolling display in a swimming pool.

CANOE RESCUE

This is a team event requiring teams of three paddlers with their canoes. On the starting signal, No. 1 of each team paddles to a given point and then capsizes. As soon as he has capsized No. 2 and No. 3 may start off. They must paddle up to the capsized canoe, empty it out, right it and assist their team mate back into his canoe. The first team of three back to the starting point are the winners. Failure to drain the capsized canoe properly disqualifies.

A variation of this is to have team of two men only, and for

17. The two-man Eskimo rescue: bow grip method (p. 147)
18. The two-man Eskimo rescue: paddle grip method (p. 148)
19, 20 & 21.   The deep water rescue (p. 146)
22, 23 & 24.   The Pawlata roll (p. 87)

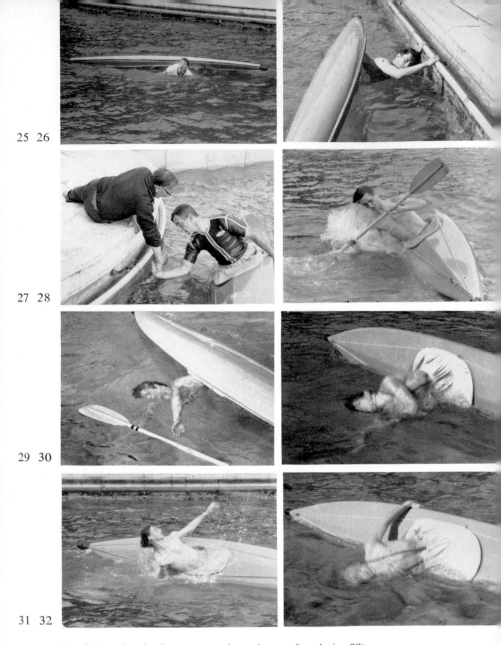

25 26

27 28

29 30

31 32

25. Swimming in the canoe and coming up for air (p. 88)
26. A confidence-building exercise
27. A teaching hand-grip which forces the canoeist to use his hips correctly
28. The Screw roll (p. 92)
29. Paddle retrieving exercise to be followed by rolling-up (p. 90)
30. The beginning of a two-handed roll with the canoe on the point of balance (p. 94)
31. Another two-handed roll. The canoeist is wasting energy by bringing up his body too fast (p. 94)
32. A one-handed roll. Note the low head position essential to success (p. 95)

the capsized canoeists to be non-competitors. In this case the capsizers take up their positions before the race and all the teams start off together.

SWIM AND RETRIEVE RACE

The canoes are taken 50 to 100 yards off shore in a lake and set adrift, or taken 50 yards upstream on a slow-moving river, and held in position by a stake boat. Competitors start from the bank, swim out to their canoes, clamber in, and paddle back to the finish.

CANOE SWAMPING CONTEST

Each canoe is equipped with a canvas or plastic bucket attached to the boat with six foot line. The object of the contest is to pour water into the other canoes until they are swamped and capsize. Touring canoes with large cockpits are best used for this. Buoyancy bags should be fitted, of course, but no spray decks.

SEEING EYE DOG RACE

For this event competitors work in teams of two, each in a single seater kayak. One member of the team is blindfolded and paddles under the direction of his sighted companion who calls out the appropriate paddling directions. The race should be over a straight course and the number of competitors should be limited so as to give each team sufficient paddling room in order to avoid collisions.

BALLOON COLLECTING CONTEST

A number of inflated balloons are released on the water some distance from the starting point. Competitors must collect as many as possible without bursting them. The winner is the paddler with the largest number of unburst balloons. When releasing the balloons attention must be paid to the wind direction.

ORGANIZING NOVELTY CANOE EVENTS
AND RAG REGATTAS

The rules for novelty events must be rather flexible and will
M

depend upon the canoes available and the type of water used. For this reason with the exception of the 'Wiggle and Wriggle Test' and 'Canoe Polo', the events outlined above have been only briefly described and are intended to provide organizers with ideas rather than rules.

The contests have been described on the assumption that single-seater kayaks will be used, since it is only in this type of craft that a paddler can learn the art of complete canoe mastery. Most of the events, of course, can be adapted for use in two-seater kayaks, or in the rare event of a club or group being able to muster sufficient Canadian canoes these could also be used. Whatever type of canoe is used, however, it is important for the organizer to check beforehand that they are in sound condition and are suited to the type of event envisaged. For example, the lightly constructed decks of the specialist long-distance racing craft should not be used for a 'Sitting on the stern race', whilst to use a standard touring canoe for the 'Wiggle' test may be challenging to the competitors it will be dull for the spectators.

This last point is important if you are organizing a fund-raising rag regatta where spectator appeal is more important than technical difficulty. Spectators will get much more excitement out of half a dozen paddlers with touring canoes racing hard in a standing position when several competitors capsize, rather than the same paddlers in narrow racing canoes moving gingerly along. Although to stand in a racing kayak may be technically more difficult.

When holding a rag regatta the organizers should plan events so that as much action as possible takes place in front of the largest part of the audience, and events should be kept sufficiently short so that attention and interest do not flag. The programme should be arranged so as to give as much variety and contrast as possible, and events where a capsize is likely should be followed by ones using different canoes, and thus avoid delay whilst canoes are brought to the shore and emptied.

In all rag regattas a rescue boat should be standing by, for although none of the events described are at all dangerous, canoeists can get into difficulties on any kind of water, and it is just possible that in the heat of competition the need for assistance may pass unnoticed unless someone is detailed to watch for such an eventuality.

The British Canoe Union Coaching Scheme—Tests and Awards

Geoff. Sanders (former BCU Hon. Coaching Secretary)

AT a time of rapid growth an activity like canoeing can soon be labelled as dangerous—'unsuitable for youngsters'—if its adherents are careless about standards of safety and performance. As the national coaching organization in this country the British Canoe Union rightly felt that it had to emphasize the need for a careful and sensible approach to the sport.

With the hope of establishing standards in canoeing the BCU introudced tests of proficiency early in 1952. Since then a whole range of tests has been instituted which caters for all degrees of ability. The Novice Test, as its name implies, is for the beginner who has reached a satisfactory standard after initial instruction. The certificate is usually awarded, free of charge, at the end of short courses as an incentive for the learner to proceed to the next stage of instruction and eventually to take the Proficiency Test. The latter can be taken on inland waters or the sea—in Canadian canoes, or kayaks. This grade could almost be likened to the motorists' driving test—the test includes what are to be considered the basic skills of the sport and it is felt that a canoeist who passes the test should be capable of handling a canoe well under most normal conditions. With the skills he has demonstrated and the application of common sense he should prove a safe canoeist.

The Advanced Tests, on the other hand, are meant for canoeists who have had considerable experience of canoeing on difficult waters. A gold badge is awarded to those proficient enough to pass the Advanced Test for the Canadian canoe and the Advanced Inland and Sea Tests for Kayaks.

The coaching scheme developed naturally from the system of tests. As more and more people took up the sport—particularly groups from schools and youth organizations—so the need for guidance and instruction grew. Sound instruction would be vital if the progress of the sport was to be along healthy lines. The scheme aimed to produce a large number of qualified canoeists for this important service.

A series of coaching awards was formulated in 1961. Instructors are qualified to teach beginners up to Proficiency Test standard. The award is open to those of 17 years of age and over—it is known that many young people make first-rate teachers. It is expected that Senior Instructors will have much greater experience of both teaching and canoeing whilst Coaches will be able to take classes of canoeists up to the Advanced Test standard and will have a very wide knowledge of all aspects of the sport. Instructors may examine for the Novice Test; Senior Instructors for the Novice and Proficiency Tests and the Instructor's Award; and Coaches for all tests and the Instructor's and Senior Awards. All are able to examine for the canoeing parts of the Duke of Edinburgh's Award and, on invitation, to test for the Boy Scouts' Association. (Coaches for the competitive branches of the sport are appointed by the specialist competitive committees of the BCU, though they come under the general coaching scheme.)

As the number of canoeists with coaching awards increased it proved possible to provide a coaching service. Many canoeists have found that they have gained considerable pleasure from introducing others to the sport and the record of work achieved has been impressive. In certain regions coaching panels, consisting of the members of the coaching scheme in an area, have been set up under the supervision of an Area Coaching Organizer. Courses and 'get-togethers' are arranged and often it is possible to provide instruction and/or examining as required. It is hoped that within a few years all regions will have their own regional coaching panels, under the general supervision of the BCU National Coaching Committee.

The National Coaching Committee is also responsible for arranging, together with the Central Council of Physical Recreation, the tours of the BCU National Coach throughout the country. His services are available to education authorities, youth organizations, colleges, schools, clubs and the like and he is able to deal with any aspect of canoeing on request. Details of the type of work he can undertake can be obtained from the BCU Hon. Coaching Secretary; requests for the use of his services should be made through the CCPR, 26 Park Cresent, London W.1.

Requests for further information about the coaching scheme, its tests and awards, or calls for assistance should be made to Mrs F. Littledyke, 15 Denewood Close, Watford, Herts. A stamped addressed envelope should be included with enquiries.

International Canoe Federation Members

CANOEISTS living or touring overseas can always obtain the latest information on local canoeing from the appropriate national canoeing organization. The list given below is of national canoeing organizations affiliated to the International Canoe Federation.

Australia   Australian Canoe Federation, 34 Hardy Terrace, East Ivanhoe, Melbourne.

Austria   Oesterreichischer paddelsportverband, Bergasse 16, Vienna IX.

Belgium   Federation Belge de canoe, Elisabethlaan, 99 Aarschot.

Bolivia   Federacion de canotaje y Remo, P.O. Box 2951, La Paz.

Bulgaria   Union Bulgare de culture physique et des sports, section de canoe et d'aviron, Boulevard Tolboukhine 18, Sofia.

Canada   Canadian Canoe Association, c/o W. Cleevely, 193 1st Street, St Lambert.

Czechoslovakia   Section Tchecoslovacque de canoe, na Porici 12, Praha 1.

Denmark   Dansk Kano og Kajak Forbund, c/o P. Rassmussen, Engelsbergvej 20 D Lyngby.

Finland   Suomen Kanoottillitto, Soutostadium, Helsinki.

France   Federation Francaise de Canoe-Kayak, 22 Avenue Victoria, Paris 1.

Germany—West Deutscher Kanu Sport Verband, Ferdinand-Wallbrechistrasse 3, Hanover.

Germany—East Deutscher Kanu-Verband, Storower Strasse 118, Berlin No. 18.

Great Britain   The British Canoe Union, 26/29 Park Crescent, London W.1.

Hungary   Magyar Kayak-Kenu Szovetset, Rosenberg Hazaspar u. 1, Budapest V.

Iran	Iranian Rowing & Yachting Federation, Fehran, Kakh, Varzesh.
Ireland	Irish Canoe Union, 33 Barnhill Road, Dalkey, Co. Dublin.
Italy	Federazioneitaliane Canottaggio, Viale Tiziano 70, Rome.
Japan	Japan Canoe Association, 25 Kannami-cho, Shibuya-ku, Tokyo
Luxembourg	Federation Luxembourgoise de Canoe-Kayak, Rue Bloch-Hausen 21, Luxembourg.
Netherlands	Nederlandsche Kano-bond, Mallewag 183, Amsterdam 18.
New Zealand	NZ Canoeing Association, c/o A. H. Carr, 0.9. Box 7068, Wellington South.
North Korea	Canoe Association of the Peoples Republic of Korea, 49 Gaisun-Dong, Moranbong District, Pysongyang.
Norway	Norges Kajak Forbund, Youngstorget 1, Oslo.
Poland	Polski Zwiazek Kajakowy, Ul. Stenkiewicza 12, Warsawa
Rumania	Federatia Romina de Sporturi nautice, Str. Vasile Conta 16, Bucuresti.
Scotland	Scottish Canoe Association, c/o D. Winning, 1 Ashburn Gardens, Gourock, Renfrewshire.
South Africa	South African Canoe Association P.O. Box 479, Vereeniging, Transvaal.
Spain	Federacion Espanola de Piraguismo, Cea Bermudez 14, 30 DP. 10–11 Madrid.
Sweden	Svenska Kanotforbundet, Biblioteksgaten 11, 111 Stokholm.
Switzerland	Schweizerischer Kanu-verband, rue Pierre Fatio, 9 Geneve.
USA	American Canoe Association, c/o Dors C. Cousin, 400 Eastern Street, New Haven, Connecticut.
USSR	The Canoe Federation of the USSR Skatertny Perenlov 4, Moscow 69.
Yugoslavia	Brodarski Savez Jugoslavije, Bulevar Revolucije 44, Beograd.

APPENDIX III

The Canoeist's Bookshelf

THE following list of books has been compiled from the recommendations of our contributors who were asked to suggest
titles which they had found interesting or useful to them as
canoeists. Books marked 'o.p.' are no longer currently available,
but can probably be obtained from public libraries.

ADNEY, E. and CHAPELLE, H.
The bark canoes and skin boats of North America. United
States National Museum, Bulletin No. 230, 1964.
A profusely illustrated anthropological study of the
canoe in N. America.

AMERICAN RED CROSS
Canoeing. American Red Cross. 1956.
The best and most comprehensive book on single-bladed
paddling, but also of value to the kayak paddler.

BLANDFORD, Percy W.
Canoes and canoeing. Lutterworth. 1962.
A good introduction with the emphasis on canoe building.

BLISS, William
Canoeing. Methuen. 1934. o.p.
A classic guide to the waterways of England and Wales
based on the author's extensive cruises.

BLISS, William
Rapid rivers. Witherby. 1935. o.p.
Really talented writing about some of the most glorious
canoeing rivers in Britain.

BRITISH CANOE UNION
Handbooks: 1. *Choosing a canoe.*
2. *Canoe handling.*
3. *Canoe camping.*
4. *Eskimo roll.*
5. *Canadian canoeing.*
6. *Long distance racing.*
These offer a convenient and efficient way of answering
the sort of questions that beginners and experts alike ask.
Under continuous revision.

BRITISH CANOE UNION
Guide to the waterways of the British Isles. British Canoe
Union. 3rd ed. 1961.
Essential for planning canoe journeys in this country.
BURNELL, Richard
The Oxford pocket book of sculling training. O.U.P. 1962.
Section three on Training can easily be adapted to the
needs of the canoeist, and will give ideas on how to train.
CHAPMAN, F. Spencer
Watkins' last expedition. Chatto. 1960. Also other editions.
An account of Gino Watkins' fateful expedition to
Greenland.
GIBSON, Charles
Be your own weatherman. Arco. 1963.
An excellent guide for the outdoor enthusiast showing
how to forecast the weather.
HORNELL, James
Water transport: origins and early evolution. C.U.P. 1946. o.p.
A fascinating and comprehensive account of small-boat
development all over the world
HUNT, Nigel
Adventures in canoeing. Pelham. 1964.
An elementary canoeing book which is controversial in
its approach, but noteworthy for the descriptive passages
which capture some of the lure and flavour of canoeing.
MacGREGOR, John
*A thousand miles in the Rob Roy canoe on the rivers and lakes
of Europe.* 13th ed. reprinted. British Canoe Union and
Canoeing Publications. 1963.
Originally published in 1866, this is the book which founded
the sport of canoeing and is still one of the best cruise
narratives.
MURRAY, Al
Modern weight training. Kaye, 1963.
An excellent book covering all aspects of weight training
including isometric muscle work.
ONTARIO VOYAGEURS KAYAK CLUB
Slalom and white water course. British edition. Canoeing
Publications. 1964.
A graduated course for the white-water canoeist which
will benefit most paddlers, and is especially valuable for
the training assignments at the end of each section.

PATTERSON, R. M.
The dangerous river. Allen and Unwin. 1954. o.p.
A vivid and stirring account of canoeing and trapping in
the North West Territories of Canada.
PHILLIPS, C. E. Lucas
Cockleshell heroes. Heinemann. 1956. o.p.
An epic of canoeing in wartime culminating in the raid on
Bordeaux harbour.
RAVEN-HART, R.
Canoe errant. Murray. 1935. o.p.
The author has probably travelled more widely by canoe
than anyone before or since. This book covers some of
his European travels; there are others describing his
voyages in America, Africa, Asia, and Australia.
SCOTT, J. M.
Gino Watkins. Hodder and Stoughton. 1935.
A study of a man who learnt to live by his kayak in
Greenland.
STATE, Oscar
Weight training for athletics. Amateur Athletic Association.
1960.
A clear and concise book which although giving exercises
for athletic events can be adapted to suit the needs of
canocists.
SUTHERLAND, Charles
Modern canoeing. Faber. 1964.
A refreshing book on canoeing which, while compre-
hensive in routine detail, puts the human side into the
centre of the picture and shares the whole wide experience
of canoeing with his reader.
VAN TIL, William
The Danube flows through Fascism. Scribner. 1938. o.p.
A 900-mile voyage by two Americans down the Danube
in a folding canoe. The book captures the charm and
interest of leisurely canoeing down a civilized waterway.
VERNEY, Michael
Complete amateur boat building. Murray. 1961.
A useful source of background material on boat building.
WHITNEY, Peter D.
White water sport. Ronald Press. 1960.
An American book which is considered to be one of the
best presentations of white water canoe sport.

Notes on the Contributors

Kathleen Tootill, for nineteen years a teacher in an experimental school and director of its company, is hon. treasurer of the Canoe Camping Club and was editor of the club's magazine, *The Canoe Camper*, 1951–64. Played hockey for Manchester University, and for the counties of Cheshire and Buckinghamshire, and was captain of the Cheshire 2nd XI. Started canoeing seriously in 1937 on the Dorset coast. Won the Women's National Slalom Championship in 1952. Helped to pioneer river canoeing in Iceland in 1957, and in Bulgaria in 1963. Has recorded more than 5,700 miles of paddling, including 1,200 miles on the sea. Is at present actively lobbying M.P.s and anyone else who can help to gain free access to the waterways of this country for canoeists.

Marianne Tucker, during the day the secretary to the managing director of a departmental store, spends most evenings either canoeing or training. She has represented Britain in the Olympic Games at Rome and Tokyo as well as at countless international regattas. Has been British Women's Champion five times. She also competes in long-distance racing where she usually paddles in the men's classes in order to find sufficient competition. She is a founder member and secretary to the group running *Canoeing* magazine. Believes that only singleness of purpose can take you to the top and keep you there. In spite of intensive training retains her femininity and has on occasion modelled for the department store in which she works.

Alan Byde was until recently a civil servant but is now at a Teacher Training College. He has built a wide range of canoes using a variety of materials and to many designs including his own. He finds endless fascination in experimenting with techniques and shapes. When not building canoes, he devotes a large part of his time to instructing newcomers to the sport. In 1962 he became an honorary senior coach of the British Canoe Union. His canoeing activities range from slalom to racing, both sprint and L.D. events, mostly at a local level, and will try his hand

at anything involving canoes. Other sports include cross-country running, rugby, swimming, cycle-racing, and judo.
Oliver Cock is the National Coach of the BCU, a post he has held since its creation in 1961. As a full-time paid official of the BCU he spends his time touring the country organizing courses and liaising with a variety of bodies such as the Royal Society for the Prevention of Accidents, and the Duke of Edinburgh's Award Schcmc. He also takes a very personal interest in the Corps of Canoe Life Guards. He has been both coach and manager of the British Slalom Team, and made a number of canoe travelogue and instructional films. He is the author of *You and Your Canoe* (1965), and with others compiled some of the BCU instructional booklets.

Jorgen Samson trained as a cartographer in the Danish Hydrographic Office, and is now acknowledged as the world's premier racing-canoe designer. Canoes to his design have won more post-war canoeing championships than those of any other designer. Started canoeing in 1935, is a Danish ex-champion and came eighth in the World Championships in 1950. He has toured extensively in Scandinavia, Germany, Austria, and Switzerland. During the war he used his skill in handling small boats to make illegal voyages by kayak and speedboat on behalf of the Resistance. Since 1946 he has designed all types of small boats. Now lives in Farum near Copenhagen in a housc on the side of a lake which enables him to go paddling every day.

Geoff. Sanders is head of the history department and senior housemaster at a Birmingham Grammar School, where he has been running a canoe club for ten years. He has been concerned with the organization of many canoe clubs, e.g. was a joint-founder of the Birmingham Canoe Club, and is Founder-Chairman of the Birmingham Schools' Canoe Association. Became the first honorary secretary of the BCU National Coaching Scheme, a position he held until 1965. He finds that introducing the sport to others is an enjoyable and challenging experience. Has strong ideas about the formation of a National Schools' Canoe Association, but has no time at the moment to implement them.

Julian Shaw is a sales representative with a large electronics firm. Started canoeing at the age of 14 when his ambition was to be in the Olympic paddling team. At 18 he went to Manchester University and was introduced to white water canoeing and became converted to this branch of the sport. He has been a member of the British Slalom Team and also British Slalom Champion. From 1957 to 1959 he was editor of *White Water*, a magazine devoted to slalom and white water canoeing. Since 1962 he has been honorary secretary of the Slalom Committee of the BCU. During the winter is an enthusiastic skier, and considers that canoes and skis are the only worthwhile means of transport.

Brian Skilling. By profession a chartered librarian. Confesses to being a dabbler, lacking the strength of purpose to pursue any branch of canoeing to its ultimate. Has dabbled in sprint racing and slalom, but prefers the leisurely business of touring. The founder and past editor of *Canoeing* magazine, he has also written *Basic Canoeing* (1963) and the BCU pamphlet on *Canadian Canoeing* (1962). In his 'spare time' he runs a canoe-training class for teachers and youth leaders in Hertfordshire.

Norman Sudron, a physical education master in a Middlesbrough school, is honorary secretary of the Middlesbrough Schools' Canoeing Association. He has been handling small boats almost all his life and has been canoeing since 1948. Although enjoying all aspects of canoeing, he finds sea work the most stimulating. He regards the canoe as being quite suitable for coastal voyaging provided the paddler is correctly trained in canoe handling and also has a sound knowledge of the action of the elements. For beach work he prefers a single-seater, but thinks that a double kayak is better for the longer sea trips.

David Sutcliffe is housemaster, head of the German department and canoe coach at Atlantic College, an international sixth-form college in South Wales. Regarded himself as being suited only to the rugby field and the fives court until spending a weekend in 1958 with canoeists from the London Federation of Boys' Clubs, under the direction of Admiral Hoare. His canoeing experience is limited to Angmagssalik kayaks and single-seater slalom boats, but this does not inhibit him from proclaiming their superiority as craft both to attract young people to the sport and in which to give them the best possible training.

Index

We draw your attention to the following advertisements, which will help you in everything connected with canoeing.

KAYE
&
WARD

*Publish books on all
these sports and games*

Angling	Hockey
Archery	Judo
Athletics	Lacrosse
Basketball	Motor Racing
Boxing	Mountaineering
Bridge	Physical Training
Camping	Riding
Canoeing	Rowing
Chess	Sailing
Cricket	Shooting
Croquet	Skating
Cycling	Skiing
Diving	Skin Diving
Draughts	Squash Rackets
Fencing	Surfing
Flying	Swimming
Football	Table Tennis
Golf	Tennis

A list will be sent on request

KAYE & WARD
194–200 Bishopsgate,
London E C 2

KAYE & WARD
also publish these fine books
on water sports

CORNELIUS SHIELDS ON SAILING
A stimulating manual for the racing sailor. Everything about choosing a racing boat, maintenance, tuning and rigging, piloting—the entire field.
10 × 7 *in., 240 pages, 44 half-tone and line illustrations. 42s.*

CRUISING *by Peter Heaton*
The companion book to *Sailing*, which covers all the more advanced navigational problems.
8¾ × 5⅝ *in., 192 pages, nearly 100 illustrations. 25s.*

THE EXPERTS' BOOK OF BOATING
Edited by Ruth Brindze
An inclusive guide to good seamanship by the world's foremost authorities.
12 × 9½ *in., 292 pages, half-tone and line illustrations. 42s.*

FASTER SAILING *by Robert N. Bavier, Jnr.*
Improvements in design and material for yacht sailing and racing.
9¼ × 6¼ *in., 196 pages, 71 photos. 21s.*

THE INTERNATIONAL BOOK OF CATAMARANS AND TRIMARANS
Compiled by Edward F. Cotter
The views and experiences of multihull sailors from all round the globe, gathered together between hard covers.
9½ × 6¼ *in., 176 pages, 166 photos, 26 drawings. 35s.*

MODERN SAILING CATAMARANS
by Robert B. Harris
The designer of the *Tigercat*, and others, explains the history, construction and sailing of 'cats'.
2nd printing 9¼ × 7 *in., 144 pages, 22 photographs and numerous diagrams. 35s.*

SAILING *by Peter Heaton*
Revised, updated edition of a 'standard' book on the subject. The new collision regulations are included; also new construction materials are described.
8¾ × 5⅝ *in., 256 pages, 16 photographs, 56 line drawings, sketches. 30s.*

SCIENTIFIC SAILBOAT RACING *by Ted Wells*
The 'classic' of small boat racing. This revised edition has been updated for English and Australian readers.
10¼ × 7¼ *in., 224 pages, 83 full page photographs and drawings. 42s.*

BETTER SWIMMING FOR BOYS AND GIRLS
by H. Elkington & Anthony Holmyard
Planned by the Amateur Swimming Association. A real contribution to swimming tuition.
9 × 7¼ *in., 96 pages, 115 photographs. 17s. 6d.*

BETTER SURFING FOR BOYS
by Joseph J. Cook & W. J. Romeika
Another 'Better Sport' book. How to choose a board, how to manipulate it—every aspect described.
8¾ × 7¾ in., 96 pages, 172 photographs; diagrams. 17s. 6d.

SURFING by H. Arthur Klein
Its history, technique—judging waves, undertows, etc.— and details of equipment. An exceptional book.
10¼ × 7¼ in., 284 pages, over 80 photographs, 34 drawings. 42s.

SWIMMING AND DIVING
by D. A. Armbruster, R. H. Allen & H. S. Billingsley
The great classic of the sport again in print and updated. Contains also a new introduction. 800 drawings were based on an underwater movie study of the world's greatest swimmers and divers. Fifth printing (revised).
9¾ × 6¾ in., 352 pages, 838 diagrams. Illustrated. 42s.

EXPLORING THE REEF
by Robert P. L. Straughan
A practical guide to the coral reef.
12 × 9½ in., 243 pages, 298 photographs (48 in full colour). 6 gns.

TEACHING SPRINGBOARD DIVING
by A. R. Fairbanks
A complete guide.
9 × 6 in., 224 pages. Illustrated. 30s.

DIVING: The Mechanics of Springboard and Firm-board Techniques
by George Eaves, B.Sc., Ph.D.
A vital book for all exponents.
8¾ × 5⅝ in., about 128 pages, 40 photographs and diagrams. 25s.

DIVE: The Complete Book of Skin Diving
by Rick and Barbara Carrier
New revised edition of a comprehensive book on the sport.
12 × 9½ in., 296 pages, 177 photographs; drawings. 50s.

UNDERWATER SWIMMING: An Advanced Handbook
by Leo Zanelli
For all those who wish to develop their skills. Detailed.
8¾ × 5⅝ in., 128 pages, 40 photographs; drawings. 30s.

MODERN SPEARFISHING by Vane Ivanovic
A comprehensive book.
Fourth edition. 8¼ × 5 in., 208 pages, 20 plates, 50 drawings. 18s.

WATER SKIING by Dick Pope, Snr.
Simple, safe fundamentals; its exciting history explained.
Second printing. 12½ × 10 in., 240 pages, 320 photographs. 35s.

HOW TO PLAY AND TEACH WATER POLO
by Charles Hines
A first-class explanatory and instructional work.
7½ × 5 in., about 128 pages. Illustrated. 15s.

The eighth edition of this invaluable book, which is now a standard reference book throughout the sporting world

OFFICIAL RULES OF SPORTS AND GAMES
1968/69

Athletics	Golf
Badminton	Hockey
Basketball	Ice Hockey
Bowls	Lacrosse
Cricket	Lawn Tennis
Croquet	Netball
Fives, Eton	Squash Rackets
Fives, Rugby	Table Tennis
Football, Association	Volleyball
Football, Rugby League	Water Polo
Football, Rugby Union	

The book is compiled with the complete co-operation of the governing association of each sport.

Educational Equipment has said of it:
'If you have anything at all to do with sport, then this is a book you simply *must* have.'

$7\frac{1}{2} \times 5$ *in.*, 730 *pages. Illustrated.* 36s.

KAYE & WARD
194–200 Bishopsgate, London EC2